THE CATHOLICITY OF THE REFORMATION

The Catholicity of the Reformation

Edited by

Carl E. Braaten and Robert W. Jenson

WILLIAM B. EERDMANS PUBLISHING COMPANY
GRAND RAPIDS, MICHIGAN / CAMBRIDGE, U.K.

© 1996 Wm. B. Eerdmans Publishing Co.
255 Jefferson Ave. S.E., Grand Rapids, Michigan 49503 /
P.O. Box 163, Cambridge CB3 9PU U.K.
All rights reserved

Printed in the United States of America

01 00 99 98 97 96   7 6 5 4 3 2 1

Library of Congress Cataloging-in-Publication Data

The Catholicity of the Reformation / edited by
Carl E. Braaten and Robert W. Jenson.
p.   cm.
Includes bibliographical references.
ISBN 0-8028-4220-8 (pbk.: alk. paper)
1. Reformation — Congresses. 2. Christian union — Congresses.
3. Church — Catholicity — Congresses. 4. Theology, Doctrinal — Congresses.
I. Braaten, Carl E., 1929-   . II. Jenson, Robert W.
BR307.C35   1996
270.6 — dc20   96-44655
                                CIP

Contents

Contents

Preface

THE TITLE of this book claims the word "catholicity" for the intent of the Reformation. The Reformers did not set out to create a new church. They aimed to reform a church that lived in continuity with the church the Creed calls "one, holy, catholic and apostolic."

The Reformation gave rise to Protestant churches that have not always understood themselves as catholic. Some Protestants have avoided the very word. Luther himself substituted "Christian" for the word "Catholic" in the Creed, lest it be equated with "Roman Catholic."

The word "catholic" was first used by St. Ignatius, who wrote to the church at Smyrna: "Wherever the bishop appears there let the congregation be, just as wherever Jesus Christ is there is the Catholic Church." The church is catholic when the living Christ is present. "Catholic" means "whole" or "total"; it derives from the Greek *kata* ("according to") and *holos* (the "whole"). The catholicity of the church includes many things: the Scriptures, apostolic tradition, sacraments, ecumenical creeds, worship, and the ministry.

There manifestly are degrees of catholicity. The full catholicity of the church — its completed integrity and comprehensiveness, its wholeness — is finally an eschatological reality in which the pilgrim church now participates through God's word and the sacraments but which she does not yet fully possess. Thus the "catholicity of the Reformation" does not point to a historical phenomenon of the sixteenth century that we would aim to repristinate; in fact the movements created by the Reformation experienced in some ways a diminishment of catholicity, such as the loss of the episcopal office. Yet this was not the intention of the Reformers. Their aim was to return to the Scriptures and ancient church tradition, to increase rather than decrease the church's catholicity.

In spite of Luther's vitriolic attacks on Rome, he never denied that it was the church catholic. In his commentary on Galatians, he wrote:

> Although the city Rome is worse than Sodom and Gomorra, nevertheless there remain Baptism, Sacraments, the Words of the Gospel, the Holy Scriptures, the Ministry of the Church, the name of Christ and the name of God. . . . Therefore, the Roman Church is holy, because she has the holy name of God, the Gospel, the Baptism, etc. If these things exist among a people, the people is called holy. Thus also our city Wittenberg is a holy city, and we are truly holy because we are baptized, have received the Holy Communion and have been taught and called by God. We have the work of God among us, the Word and the Sacraments, and these make us holy.[1]

From the beginning there have been evangelical catholic movements within Protestantism harking back to Luther's original intention. The leader of one such, Friedrich Heiler, wrote typically: "It was not Luther's idea to set over against the ancient Catholic Church a new Protestant creation; he desired nothing more than that the old Church should experience an evangelical awakening. . . . Luther and his friends wished, as they were never tired of emphasizing, to be and to remain Catholic."[2] Such movements held to the reformed Roman mass and other forms of Catholic worship and piety — matins and vespers, confession and absolution, liturgical vestments, the use of incense, the sign of the cross, and so on.

The rationalistic blight of the Enlightenment, with its withering attack on everything "medieval," destroyed such continuities in much of Protestantism. The nineteenth century witnessed several reactions to Enlightenment Protestantism. One was the evangelical awakenings that sought to restore traditional forms of piety centered in Bible reading, family devo-

---

1. Martin Luther, *Lectures on Galatians 1535, Luther's Works,* trans. by Jaroslav Pelikan (St. Louis: Concordia Publishing House, 1963), vol. 26, pp. 24-25.

2. Friedrich Heiler, "The Catholic Movement in German Lutheranism," in *Northern Catholicism: Centenary Studies in the Oxford and Parallel Movements,* ed. N. P. Williams and Charles Harris (London: SPCK, 1933), p. 478.

tions, private prayer, and revival. Another was the attempt to restore the confessional substance of the Reformation, led by such personalities as Friedrich J. Stahl, August F. C. Vilmar, and Wilhelm Löhe. A high church movement embraced Friedrich Schelling's vision of a coming "evangelical catholicism": Catholicism ("the Petrine church") and Protestantism ("the Pauline church") will be synthesized in a church both evangelical and catholic ("the Johannine church"). Schelling's idealistic philosophy of history greatly influenced Philip Schaff and John Nevin, leaders of the Mercersburg theology of "Protestant Catholicism."

The high church movement of evangelical catholics in Germany defined itself ecumenically in relation to Orthodox, Anglican, and Roman Catholic Christians in Germany. It created the Evangelical Catholic Eucharistic Society, dedicated to creating an inner synthesis between Catholic dogma and worship and the Lutheran emphasis on justification by grace through faith. It stressed that "evangelical" and "catholic" are not contradictory, but blend harmoniously in a comprehensive vision of the one holy church. It worked and prayed for union with the Roman Catholic Church and the Orthodox Churches, while not neglecting relations with Anglo-Catholics and similar groups within European Calvinism.

For many years the chief organ of high church Lutherans in America was a journal entitled *Una Sancta.* Indeed, in some loose sense this journal was the spiritual predecessor of *Pro Ecclesia,* the journal of the Center for Catholic and Evangelical Theology. The great difference is that *Una Sancta* was a Lutheran journal, whereas *Pro Ecclesia* is an ecumenical journal, supported by theologians of many traditions.

In his own way Paul Tillich often called attention to the catholicity of the Reformation, when he spoke of the need for "the Protestant principle" to maintain dynamic connection with "the Catholic substance." Tillich's concept of the "Protestant principle" intended to convey what lay at the center of the teaching of Paul, Augustine, and Luther: justification by grace through faith. Justification, according to Tillich, is not only a doctrine among others, "but also a principle, because it is the first and basic expression of the Protestant principle itself."[3] As a principle, justification should permeate "every single assertion of the theological system."[4] But precisely

3. Paul Tillich, *Systematic Theology* (Chicago: University of Chicago Press, 1963), vol. 3, p. 223.

4. Tillich, p. 224.

as a principle it cannot stand alone; it cannot by itself provide the basis and content of the Christian faith. What is needed is "the Catholic substance"; this is the concrete embodiment of Christ, mediated by the living institutional and sacramental realities of the church in history. Protestant principle without its Catholic substance would be "empty"; Catholic substance without the Protestant principle would be "blind."

Throughout the modern period Swedish theologians have been particularly aware of the Catholicity of the Reformation. Nathan Söderblom suggested that "three principal divisions of Christianity should be called Greek Catholic, Roman Catholic, and Evangelical Catholic."[5] He believed that it was incorrect to reserve the name "catholic," as had become customary in popular usage, for the Church of Rome. Gustaf Aulén, continuing in the line of Nathan Söderblom, wrote that "there can be no doubt about the *will* of the Reformation to certify its catholicity, or more correctly the catholicity of the church."[6] He warned against seeing the relation of Protestantism to Catholicism mainly in terms of contrast. By defining itself as anti-Catholic, Protestantism progressively loses essentials of the faith confessed in the Creeds.

Most chapters of this book originated as addresses given at a conference on "The Catholicity of the Reformation," held by the Center for Catholic and Evangelical Theology at St. Olaf College, October 23-24, 1994, and at Grace Lutheran Church, Lancaster, Pennsylvania, October 30-31, 1994. The conference called heirs of the Reformation, churches and pastors, to be faithful to both the evangelical and catholic elements of the great Christian tradition. We are grateful that William B. Eerdmans Publishing Company, by publishing this volume, will broaden the audience far beyond the hundreds who attended.

Carl E. Braaten
Robert W. Jenson

5. Quoted by Gustaf Aulén, *Reformation and Catholicity,* trans. Eric H. Wahlstrom (Philadelphia: Muhlenberg, 1961), p. 177.
6. Aulén, p. 193.

The Church as *Communio*

Robert W. Jenson

I

THE SO-CALLED *communio* ecclesiology has since the second Vatican Council become a major achievement of ecumenical consensus. The consensus is first between East and West; here it is very much a matter of Western assent to positions that the East anciently treasured and has recently again come to emphasize. But these Eastern positions have also shown the power to transcend inner-Western barriers and provide Catholics and Protestants with shared ecclesiology — indeed, one must note the extraordinary influence of one book, John Zizioulas's *Being as Communion*.

The *communio* ecclesiology has two parts. One is a doctrine of the church's ontological foundation. In order both to give a first statement of the doctrine and to show its ecumenical status, let me cite two consensus statements. The first is the text approved by a joint Roman Catholic–Orthodox Commission at Munich in 1982: "The church finds its model, its origin and its end in the mystery of the one God in three persons. . . . This mystery of the unity in love of plural persons properly constitutes the newness of the trinitarian *koinonia* which is communicated to humans in the church."[1] The other is the document that in 1980 concluded the decisive round of international Catholic-Lutheran dialogue: the church's unity is

---

1. *The Mystery of the Church and the Eucharist in the Light of the Mystery of the Holy Trinity*, II.2.

"created in the image and likeness of the Triune God" and is "lived in personal fellowship with the Triune God."[2]

The other part of the *communio* ecclesiology is a doctrine of the church's structure. Its classic statement is in *Lumen gentium* itself, where the one church is said to consist *in et ex* the many churches. But here, too, I can cite the dialogues. The East-West dialogue states: "Most profoundly, because the one and only God is the communion of three Persons, the one and unique church is a communion of many communities and the local church a communion of persons."[3] Catholic-Protestant dialogue states, in a document of 1985: "The church is therefore a communion *(communio)* subsisting in a network of local churches."[4]

What I will try to do in this paper is both report something of existing ecumenical thinking and develop it where it seems clear to me how this ought to be done. It will, I fear, often not be very clear where the one ends and the other begins, since this distinction is no longer very clear to me.

II

The church is founded in the triune life of God because the church anticipates being taken into that life, and because, as the gospel interprets reality, it is precisely what creatures may *anticipate* from God that is their deepest being.

In the New Testament, three descriptions of the church are decisive and compendious: the church is the people of God, the church is the body of Christ, and the church is the temple of the Spirit. In all three cases, the church exists only by anticipation. God's one people will not gather until the last day; therefore the church can now be the one people of God only in anticipation of that gathering. The church is the body of that Christ whose bodily departure to God's right hand his disciples once witnessed, and whose return in like fashion we must still await. The church is the temple of that Spirit whose very reality among us is "down payment," *arrabon.*

2. *Ways to Community,* 44-45.
3. *The Mystery of the Church and the Eucharist in the Light of the Mystery of the Holy Trinity,* III.2.
4. *Facing Unity,* 5.

Just so, the church is grounded in God himself, who is the *Eschatos,* the one who can only be anticipated. All God's creatures are moved by God to their fulfillment in him; the church is doubly so moved, as one among God's creatures and as the creature that mediates the movement for others. Paul's saying is both cosmic and ecclesiological: "Then comes the end, when he delivers the kingdom to God the Father . . . , that God may be *panta en pasin* [all in all]" (1 Cor. 15:24, 28).

The patristic concept of *theosis* is the most precise and compendious possible evocation of the end for which God creates us. The difference of Creator and creature is indeed absolute and eternal, but precisely because God is the infinite Creator there can be no limit to the modes and degrees of creatures' promised participation in his life. And it is of God's *life* that we here have to think. Our end is not participation in an abstract essence of Godhead, but in the life that Father, Son, and Spirit have among themselves.

Thus all being other than God is anticipation of its own participation in God's being. Foundationally to that relation and specifically to our purpose, all *koinonia* is founded and defined in the *koinonia* that, under the traditional label *perichoresis,* is the life of the triune God. The triune hypostases, Father, Son, and Spirit, do not merely have fellowship one with another; they are real as and only as the poles of that fellowship. As the great scholastic formula says, a triune hypostasis simply is a "relation subsisting."[5] Yet precisely so the triune hypostases subsist genuinely, as identities capable of fellowship. As the communion that is God, their communion is at once infinitely intimate and infinitely comprehensive; therefore they can even make room among them for others. And by God's free choice, that room is opened to created persons, and the church is taken to be those persons.

In the great biblical scene in which many Fathers most distinctly perceived God as Trinity,[6] the baptism of the Lord, the Father speaks love to the Son, the Son submits to the Father, and the Spirit appears as the hypostatic gift of their communication (Mark 1:9-11 and par.). Here both the personal discourse and meeting between Father and Son and Spirit and their unity in action and being are equally manifest. And then we should note how Matthew directs the Father's word of love for the Son also to

5. Thomas Aquinas, *Summa theologiae,* 1,29,a.4.
6. E.g., Tertullian, *Against Praxeas,* xi,9-10.

3

those who are to hear the Son, how the loving converse of the Trinity opens to disciples (Matt. 3:13-17).

When the gospel of Christ's resurrection is audibly and visibly spoken by and heard in the church, it is — in anticipation — the very word of the Father to the Son that we hear; thus the church's mission is founded in the inner-triune sending of the Son by the Father. When the church prays to the Father in the Son's name, the church is taken into the very obedience of the Son to his sending by the Father. As the church speaks and hears the gospel and as the church responds in prayer and confession, the church's life is a great conversation, and this conversation is none other than our anticipatory participation in the converse of the Father and the Son in the Spirit; as the church is enlivened and empowered by this hearing and answer, this inspiration is by none other than that Spirit who is the life between the Father and the Son.

III

The second part of the *communio* ecclesiology derives from the first. It is the trinitarian and eschatological quality of the church's fellowship that determines that this fellowship is at once the gathered fellowship of believers and the fellowship among such gatherings. Because the persons of the triune God are one God, and because the believers who meet in local fellowship assemble with the Son, before the Father, and therefore in the Father's Spirit which rests on the Son, these believers are one. And because their fellowship is thus founded in the one God, there can finally be only one such fellowship: one people and one body and one temple. But only at the end can this entire fellowship assemble face-to-face; between the times, each local fellowship can know itself as the one church of God only in fellowship with all those other fellowships that know themselves in the same way and with which it will at the end be joined.

To quote ecumenical documents once again: "The one church of Jesus Christ assumes concrete form in local churches which participate in the diversity of historical, cultural and racial situations in which the people live to whom the gospel is proclaimed in word and sacrament. The church is therefore a communion *(communio)* subsisting in a network of local churches."[7]

7. *Facing Unity,* 5.

IV

So much for the very broadest strokes. For a slightly more detailed analysis of ecclesial *koinonia,* the great opening blessing of 1 John can be a first motto: "that you may have fellowship with us; and our fellowship is with the Father and with his Son Jesus Christ"(1:3). The *koinonia* that is the church is not foundationally our association with one another. The *koinonia* that is the church is foundationally our fellowship with God in the incarnate Christ; then, because our participation in God is participation in the triune God whose very being is *koinonia,* our joint participation in God becomes our participation with one another.

It is *baptism* that creates the community of the church, with its shared blessings, and brings each of us into that community. The church is the community of the justified and sanctified; thus baptism's work is described in the New Testament as justification and sanctification (1 Cor. 6:11). The church is a priestly and prophetic community; in the New Testament, baptism is invoked as the anointing by which priests and prophets are made (Heb. 10:22; 1 John 2:20). The church is persecuted but victorious; according to the New Testament, baptism "saves"(1 Pet. 1:3-21). And this same baptism is foundationally initiation into the fellowship of Christ's disciples and just so into God's triunity (Matt. 28:19); indeed, it is incorporation into the risen Christ's own body and into dying and rising with and in him (Rom. 6:1-11).

These relationships, constituted in baptism, are enacted in the church's celebration of eucharist, of "the" communion. The apostle Paul in his first letter to the Corinthians can be our guide. "The cup of blessing which we bless, is it not a *koinonia* in the blood of Christ? The bread which we break, is it not a *koinonia* in the body of Christ? Because there is one bread, we who are many are one body, for we all partake *(metechomen)* of the one bread" (10:16-17). One occasion of his writing to the Corinthians was their violation of this unity. Thus the dialectics of Paul's following rebuke (11:27-29) precisely trace the dialectics of Christian communion. At their celebrations, the Corinthians violated their fellowship with one another by individualistic pursuit of blessings, and by that very action profaned the body of the Lord. We may ask, Which body of the Lord? The bread and cup or the congregation? But it is plain: Paul intends both at once, in dynamic identity.

For the ancient church, Paul's doctrine of *koinonia* in Christ provided the chief paradigm of self-understanding. John of Damascus summarized centuries of patristic interpretation: "[The Eucharist] is called *koinonia* and truly it is. For through it we both commune *(koinonein)* with Christ, and share in his body as well as in his deity, and commune *(koinonein)* and are united with one another. For because we all eat of one loaf we become one body and one blood of Christ and members of one another; we may be said to be embodied with Christ *(sussomoi tou christou)*."[8]

Nor was the New Testament church's grasp of itself as *koinonia* limited to the fellowship within local congregations. Notoriously, *ekklesia* in the New Testament — and notably precisely in 1 Corinthians — can denote a local fellowship, or it can denote all such fellowships as a class, or it can denote all such fellowships as one great fellowship (1 Cor. 1:2; 7:17; 12:28).

Also this aspect of *koinonia* became determinative for the self-understanding of the ancient church. The prayer recorded in the *Didache* summons all believers "from the four corners of the earth" to the local eucharist.[9] That the local gathering is thus in its self-understanding identical with the one gathering of all must, moreover, find expression in practiced fellowship; in the ancient church this was accomplished by the solemn and carefully granted exchange of communicants and celebrants between local fellowships.

V

My discussion of churchly *koinonia* has so far been predominantly christological. Within Western tradition, this is not to be regretted; nor is it ever right to set "christological" and "trinitarian" against each other, for the christological and trinitarian doctrines are but one and the same interpretation of God. But now I want to try to show how churchly *koinonia* is grounded also in the doctrines of the Spirit and of the Father.

The baptismal creeds speak of the *church* just as they come to confess the *Spirit*, for it is as God's people confess God as Spirit that we come to our own communal place in such confession. Every living community has its spirit, the bond through which members draw life from each other and

8. *The Orthodox Faith* IV,13.
9. *Didache*, X,5.

are free for each other; it is the mystery of the church that God's Spirit is the church's spirit.

Thus we come again to the wellspring of the church's *koinonia:* to baptism. In the witness of Scripture, the decisive difference between Christian baptism and all earlier ordinances is that baptism bestows the Spirit (Mark 1:8 and par.; Acts 10:1-7). And in all our variety, there is but one Spirit into which we are baptized (1 Cor. 12:13). It is precisely in this unity, consisting in the Spirit and granted in baptism, that the rich mutuality of the church's fellowship is founded (12:12).

Just so also we come again to the *goal* of Christian fellowship. In the New Testament, the church is the community sanctified, anointed, and saved by baptism. But all this language for the efficacy of baptism is eschatological; each of the church's blessings is a specific anticipation of life in the kingdom of God. And it is precisely therein that they can all together be evoked as the gift of the Spirit, for the Spirit is the present Energy of the end, the Liveliness of a community whose whole life is hope for the fulfillment of God's promises (2 Cor. 1:22; 5:5; Eph. 1:14). The goal of that *koinonia* which is the church is the *koinonia* of the kingdom; the Spirit is the reality of the first because he is the reality of the second. And all this again may be taken together in the great saying of Paul: "Now the Lord is the Spirit, and where the Spirit of the Lord is, there is freedom. And we all . . . , beholding the glory of the Lord, are being changed into his likeness . . . ; for this comes from the Lord who is the Spirit" (2 Cor. 3:17-18).

The kingdom is not the fulfillment of the church only, but of all creation, and so of that "world" in which the church lives. Therefore, as the church lives in anticipation of the kingdom, the church not only is community, but creates community beyond itself. The effects in the world of the gospel's preaching are not fully predictable and are not exhausted in the recruitment of the church to carry on the preaching. What can be predicted is that where the church's mission is in any way effective, there *koinonia* will appear. This, too, is a work of the Spirit.

Precisely as the church shares in the life of all the triune hypostases, the church shares in the relation of the Son and the Spirit to the *Father.* As the Son and the Spirit come forth *from* the Father, so the dynamic of their existence is *toward* the Father. And so, too, the body of the Son and the community of the Spirit live toward the Father. An ellipsis in an earlier citation from the apostle Paul must here be restored: "Then comes the end, when he delivers the kingdom to God the Father. . . . When all things are subjected to him, then the Son himself will also be subjected to him who put all things under him, that God may be *panta en pasin* [all in all]" (1 Cor. 15: 24, 28). The great goal of our *koinonia,* to which the Spirit draws us, is the Father's kingdom.

Therefore the church as it is determined by the Father's triune role is above all a *koinonia* of *prayer.* The church gathers with the Son and in the Spirit, to petition and adore the Father. As the christological and pneumatological center of the church's *koinonia* is the eucharist, so the central act of the church at eucharist is the "Great Thanksgiving" or *Anaphora,* in which the church recites and glorifies the saving actions that the Father has performed in the Son by the Spirit, and in which the church gives its praises the explicit form of the triune relations, as praise, *anamnesis,* and *epiclesis.*

It is on this pattern that the church lives in the world. If the church's christological and pneumatological realities can be comprehended as its mission, so the church's specific reality vis-à-vis the Father is its *intercession.* Agitated by the Spirit and implicated, as the Son's body, with all creation as it is made through and for the Son, the church's petition and praise represent before the Father the petition and praise of all creation.

That is to say, the church's vocation before the Father is *priestly,* and the church's service before him *sacrificial.* At eucharist and throughout the church's life, the church *offers* petition and praise, with the Son and in the Spirit, to the Father. "When you pray," our Lord taught us, "pray so: Our Father. . . ." And we dare do so because when we do, there he is in our midst, praying with and through us.

Our petition and praise are offered indeed as *words* of petition and praise; but at eucharist and throughout the church's life, these words are *embodied* words. The insight of St. Augustine is foundational for the whole Western church: the Word of God is essentially audible *and* "visible," heard *and* "seen"; it is never content to be language only but takes to itself "elements" of the visible world, gestures and objects, to become itself "visible word." This insight cannot apply only to God's word to us, to make God's word "sacramental." It must also apply to that word which God the Spirit speaks through us to the Father (Rom. 8:26); it must apply to the church's petition and praise. But embodied prayer, prayer with words and with gestures and objects, is what in the church's long tradition has been called "sacrifice."

8

VI

We turn again to the way *communio* ecclesiology understands the church's polity. The local church is a communion of persons; "higher" levels of the church's gathering, patriarchal or national or perhaps even denominational churches, are communions of local communions; and the one catholic church is the communion of all churches.

We have just discussed how churchly communion is in all its aspects sacramental and sacrificial. It follows that the structure proper to the church is the structure proper to its sacramental life. The center of the continuing communion of the church is the eucharist. Therefore the communion of local churches with each other is foundationally their eucharistic fellowship, their sharing of the Supper with one another; and the communion of the one church is nothing but a universal fellowship of the eucharist. The polity of the church is then the structure by which eucharistic fellowship is enabled and bounded; and the right polity of the church will be a structure appropriate to this purpose.

It is always the role and status of the ordained ministry that is the heart of a churchly polity; this is true also of free-church or even anticlerical polities. It is surely clear what ordained ministry must be by the lights of the *communio* ecclesiology. Moreover, there exists broad ecumenical consensus in the doctrine of ordained ministry; and this consensus exactly matches what the *communio* ecclesiology demands. By the lights of this ecclesiology, the ordained ministry must be fundamentally a "ministry of unity": persons are ordained to be *pastors*, shepherds, of the flock's mutuality, of its *koinonia*.

This is true in the local church. It is, to be sure, ecumenically disputed what exactly is to count as the local church. Protestants are likely to think first of the *parish* as the fundamental local unit; Catholics think first of the *diocese*, the larger congregation that is already in itself a communion of communions. The matter is surely reconcilable. In effect, Protestants think of the parish pastor as a bishop, and Catholics think of the bishop as the pastor of a complex parish.

Either way, the bishop/pastor is first and foremost the shepherd of a flock that belongs together but tends to stray. And the place where this unity becomes actual and therefore is to be tended is the eucharist. The center of the pastoral office and so of the ordained ministry is presidency at the eucharist.

9

The same is true of the communion of local communions. Whether we call those who tend churchly communion "pastors" or "bishops," they are the ministers also of this unity. It is exactly their communion with one another, their mutual recognition of one another's local communities, that constitutes the communion of communions.

Two mandates surely have force at this point, both of which would be satisfied by a right churchly polity, but which historically have been in some conflict with each other. First, what is often called the *collegiality* simply of the pastors or bishops with each other is what establishes churchly unity. Second, the communion thus constituted needs its *own pastor,* its own minister of unity. So in a standard episcopal polity, every parish has two pastors: its priest and its bishop. The priest serves as the parish's own pastor and the bishop as the pastor of the larger though still local communion within which the parish has its place. Moreover, these mandates repeat themselves at however many further levels of churchly communion there are or should be.

Two final points must be made either briefly or at great length. I choose brevity. First, the ecclesiology just sketched obviously suggests the necessity of a pastor of the one universal church, a shepherd of *its* unity. One ought not to adopt the *communio* ecclesiology without considering this. Second, insofar as there is ecumenical or innerconfessional dispute about the *communio* ecclesiology, the center of argument has been the place of legal authority, of "jurisdiction." For example, between East and West, can the bishop of Rome be recognized as universal pastor but *not* as universally exercising legal authority?

VII

It will have been noted that I have been treading more and more dangerous ecumenical ground. At the end — and the pun is intended — a discussion of the church as *koinonia* cannot avoid a matter on which there is very little consensus indeed — but where I am myself convinced that there is also very little justification for dissensus.

If the *communio* ecclesiology so far developed in this essay is at all correct, we cannot avoid going on to confess that the church is *communio sanctorum* also in the sense that the church is an *eschatologically inclusive* fellowship of those made holy by faith. As we are in the church in fellowship one with another, we are just thereby in fellowship with all believers, from the beginning of the pilgrimage of God's people to its consummation. Neither death nor yet the hiddenness of the future can sever the fellowship of the saints, for the *koinonia* of the church is participation in the eternal inner *koinonia* of the triune God, and is constituted in that Spirit who is the very Power of life. The teaching of Vatican II seems to me simply true: "The union of the wayfarers with the brethren who sleep in the peace of Christ is in no way interrupted, but on the contrary . . . , this union is reinforced by a communion *(communicatio)* of spiritual goods."[10]

Such eschatologically inclusive *koinonia* is also founded in the mystery of the triune God. It is itself a mystery, which we can penetrate conceptually only to a limited degree. Exactly wherein does the "communion of spiritual goods" just affirmed consist? And how may we practice it? Over against the eschatological limit faced by such questions, churches have sometimes gone differing ways, more in liturgy and piety than in formulated doctrine.

Much polemic between Catholic and Protestant in this matter has been occasioned more by the difficulty of interpreting unfamiliar pious practice than by necessary theological contradiction. We should note how carefully the adversarial documents of the sixteenth century state their formal teachings, despite the general vehemence of their polemics on this point. Thus the *Apology of the Augsburg Confession* first affirms that the saints in heaven do indeed pray as a body for the church on earth.[11] Then it argues that since Scripture does not tell us that individual saints can be addressed by those on earth, it is illegitimate to command us to invoke them.[12] But just this is what the Council of Trent carefully refrains from doing, laying down no obligation individually to invoke the saints, and decreeing only that it is "good and useful" *(bonum atque utile)* to do so, and that those who *forbid* it "entertain an impious opinion" *(impie sentire).*[13]

Such observations do not, to be sure, constitute an ecumenical agreed interpretation of the "communion of spiritual goods" between the church on earth and the church in heaven. Yet the following can surely be said.

As the fellowship of the church is foundationally fellowship with Christ, so the fellowship of the church on earth with the church in heaven

10. *Lumen gentium,* 49.
11. *Apology of the Augsburg Confession,* XXI, 8-9.
12. *Apology of the Augsburg Confession,* XXI, 10-13.
13. *Canones et decreta dogmatica,* Sess. XXV, "De invocatione. . . ."

is foundationally fellowship with Christ. The saints in heaven are not our way to Christ; Christ is our way to them. Our converse with them, however the mystery of that converse is to be practiced, is not fundamentally different from our converse with one another, as in the proclamation of the gospel we speak for Christ and hearken to one another as to Christ, or as we join in the table fellowship of his body and blood. And as we can be tempted to make the fellowship of saints on earth its own foundation, in tension with our fellowship with Christ, so can we be tempted with respect to our fellowship with saints in heaven; here as elsewhere, however, the right cure for abuse cannot be abolition of the use.

Insofar as the Catholic church, with its richer veneration of the saints, takes to heart the admonition of *Lumen gentium,* "Let us teach the faithful . . . that the authentic cult of the saints does not consist so much in a multiplicity of external acts, but rather in a more intense practice of our love, whereby, for our own greater good and that of the Church, we seek from saints 'example in their way of life, fellowship in their communion, and the help of their intercession,'"[14] the occasion of much earlier offense is removed. And insofar as Catholics thus provide a pure example of experienced fellowship with saints in heaven, Protestants should be moved to its freer practice.

14. *Lumen gentium,* 15.

The Catholic Luther

David S. Yeago

I

I WANT TO propose a way of reading Luther that runs counter to the way in which much twentieth-century Protestant Luther scholarship has interpreted him. Inevitably, I have to begin with a disclaimer: I naturally cannot hope to offer here a proper *argument* that my way of reading Luther is better than the usual way. To do that would require offering extended readings of large tracts of his writing to show that the way I propose to interpret him makes better sense of the texts, accounts better for what he actually says, than other interpretations. I hope in fact to offer such an extended argument in the near future, but here I have no alternative but to proceed in a more or less assertorial mode. I will present a proposal that I hope may stimulate a return to Luther's texts to see things that are obscured by many standard interpretations. I will, so to speak, describe the shoe; readers may let Luther wear it if they find that it fits him.

Translations of Luther in this essay are by the author. References in the text are to *D. Martin Luthers Werke. Kritische Gesamtausgabe* (Weimar 1883ff.) [*WA*]. In the case of the *Heidelberg Disputation* reference is made to the superior critical text presented by Helmar Junghans in Martin Luther, *Studienausgabe,* vol. 1, ed. Hans-Ulrich Delius (Berlin, 1979) [*Studienausgabe*].

II

What might be called the standard Protestant way of reading Luther is dominated by a particular story about Luther's development as a theologian up to his open break with the Roman Church. That story goes something like this: from the very beginning, the young Luther was haunted by a question for which traditional catholic Christianity could provide no answers. This question arose from Luther's deep religious or existential — you can choose your preferred jargon — insight into the truth of the human condition before God, which was systematically distorted by traditional Christianity.

Theologically expressed, this insight consisted of a deep sense of the inauthenticity of all our works before God; thus Luther could find no lasting peace in the edifice of catholic faith and practice, organized as it was around sacramental practice, dogmatic faith, and mystical aspiration, for these were in the last analysis only denials of the truth of our condition, not satisfying responses to it. In none of these could Luther find an answer to the question that drove him, which was, of course, the famous question, How can I get a gracious God?

At this point, there are two ways of continuing the story. Some scholars believe that Luther found his distinctive answer to this question very early, even before his first surviving academic lectures, and that his subsequent development as a theologian was a matter of bringing his crucial discovery gradually to sufficiently clear expression that it finally provoked the inevitable conflict with the defenders of traditional Christianity.

However, since the Second World War, most Luther scholars have come to tell the story a little differently. They believe that Luther found the answer to his driving existential question only in 1518, after the indulgence controversy was already under way. His development up to that point must therefore be understood as the story of his ongoing struggle with the question "How can I get a gracious God?" Because this question all by itself struck at the roots of traditional catholic Christianity, Luther's persistence in asking it was enough to get him in hot water. But after the "Reformation discovery" of 1518 the handwriting was on the wall; Luther and those who were captivated by his gospel could no longer live in the house of catholic tradition.

III

I believe that the second group of scholars, who are the majority today, are quite right to say that something decisive happened in Luther's thinking in the year 1518, and so it is their version of the story to which I will be responding. But it is important that we pause for a moment and consider some of the broader implications of either version of this way of telling Luther's story.

First of all, on either account, Luther's so-called "Reformation break-through" is implicitly construed as a full-scale *refounding of Christianity,* on a par in most important respects with Pentecost. To be sure, most interpreters of Luther would probably not feel comfortable saying this in so many words, but it is the inescapable implication of the way the story is often told. Consider the language used: Luther's breakthrough is said to have been a "rediscovery of the gospel." This surely implies that the gospel got lost somehow between Pentecost and the Reformation, and so had to be revealed again. And what is the revelation of the gospel if not the founding of Christianity and of the church?

Furthermore, this construal of Luther's story implies that Luther stands in no significant relationship to the preceding Christian tradition. Luther's Reformation breakthrough, it is assumed, came about by way of a pure encounter of the naked human condition with the naked Pauline *kerygma,* mediated by no diachronic historical process. Luther is read as saying something *radically* different from everything in the church's tradition from the death of Paul to the Tower Experience, except perhaps for a few glimmers in Augustine. The catholic tradition figures in the story only as that which Luther had to overcome, to "break through," on his way to "rediscovering the gospel." It follows that those who are concerned with Luther have little reason for overmuch concern with that tradition; it often appears in the literature in the form of broad, stereotypical descriptions of "scholasticism" or "mysticism" or "traditional dogma" that serve as a foil for Luther's "discovery."

One outcome of this, by the way, is that the academic industry of modern Luther study has done less than one might suppose to illumine Luther's relationship to patristic and medieval thought — naturally enough, if the interpretive project is proceeding under the assumption that any ties to that history are necessarily superficial, affecting the surface but not the depths of his thought. Only so can we explain why, for example, after a century of academic *Lutherforschung,* we are only beginning to get precise and thorough accounts of Luther's debt, which in my judgment is rather plainly enormous, to Bernard of Clairvaux.

A final implication of this way of reading Luther is the most important and the most troubling: the sixteenth-century schism is construed as the logical, inevitable, and *necessary* public outcome of Luther's theological development. If even Luther's question was simply impossible for traditional catholic Christianity to assimilate, much less the answer he discovered; if Luther's "faith" was something different in kind from the faith of catholic Christianity, then of course, obviously, a new faith demanded and got a new church. No veneer of ecumenical courtesy can change the fact that on this reading of Luther, the two parties to the schism were in effect practicing different religions. Ecumenically, therefore, this way of telling Luther's story is quite conservative in its effects, even though it presents Luther as a radical, because it functions as a legitimation of things as they are; it makes the present division of the church seem normal and inevitable to us.

The reading of Luther that I want to propose flies quite deliberately in the face of all these implications. While something important for Luther's theological development did occur in 1518, it was not a "Reformation turn" to an insight that led ineluctably away from the catholic tradition. On the contrary, it is better described as a *catholic turn* that anchored the concerns and insights of Luther's early work much more solidly than before *within* the framework of catholic Christianity. Moreover, Luther's theology from start to finish was much more deeply shaped than we have realized by his scholastic, monastic, and patristic predecessors; he was creative, but his creativity lay especially in his fresh grasp of traditional problems and in his innovative integration and use of traditional resources to address those problems.

Of course, if all this is so, then we will no longer be able to suppose that the Reformation schism makes sense because the Reformers had discovered a radically new version of Christianity for which the old church couldn't make room. On the reading I will propose, there is no grand, consoling reason for the way the Reformation turned out; the schism with which we are living is nothing more or less than a sorry mess, brought about by contingent human choices in a confused historical context defined less by clear and principled theological argument (though, of course, that was present) than by a peculiar (and distinctively sixteenth-century) com-

16

bination of overheated and ever-escalating polemics, cold-blooded *Real-politik*, and fervid apocalyptic dreaming.

IV

If one looks carefully at what Luther actually wrote in the period up to 1517-1518 (as distinguished from his reminiscences twenty or twenty-five years later), one discovers that the celebrated question "How can I get a gracious God?" is rather conspicuous by its absence. That is to say, the driving issue in Luther's early theology was not, on the face of it, the problem of the assurance of forgiveness or the certitude of salvation.

There was, to be sure, a pastoral problem of the "troubled conscience" in the late medieval church, brought about (to oversimplify rather drastically) by the convergence of certain unresolved issues in Augustine's theology of grace with certain developments in the canon law of penance. It is well to remember, though, that the "troubled conscience" was never a simple and uniform spiritual malaise, but took very different specific forms in different pastoral and theological contexts. The young Luther did almost certainly suffer from a "troubled conscience" in *some* form, but the clearest evidence of any awareness on his part of the problem of assurance is his occasional insistence that we *cannot* be certain of God's forgiveness, and that this uncertainty plays an important and ultimately positive role in God's dealings with us. Whatever the role played by a "troubled conscience" in the young Luther's life, it evidently did not cause his theological work to be dominated by the question "How can I get a gracious God?"

There is, in fact, a driving question in Luther's early theology, but it is not the question of the assurance of forgiveness. The troubling question that emerges from the preoccupations of the young Luther's thought is not "How can I get a *gracious* God?" but "Where can I find the *real* God?" All the evidence in the texts suggests that it was the threat of *idolatry*, not a craving for assurance of forgiveness, that troubled Luther's conscience if anything did. And this question did not, as some of Luther's interpreters have been eager to believe, burst the framework of traditional Christianity; both the emergence of the problem itself and Luther's eventual solution to it locate him precisely within the catholic tradition.

At its heart, Luther's early theology is marked by a strong emphasis on what the scholastics called *uncreated grace*, grace as the presence of the uncreated God, and on the transformation of the human heart by the presence of God in the utter transcendence of his godhead. Much of Luther's criticism of contemporary theology focused on the way in which it *naturalized* grace, played down its radically transformative and inevitably disruptive impact on human normalcy. In this, Luther was not breaking with catholic tradition but self-consciously retrieving the tradition, bringing to bear the deepest insights of Augustine and the great monastic teachers on a scholasticism out of touch with its own roots.

The effect of such radically transformative grace, according to the Augustinian tradition and the young Luther, is that the heart adheres to God and loves God above all things *for God's own sake;* in Augustine's terms, we come to *enjoy* God and *use* created things for God's sake, rather than attempting to "use" God for the sake of created enjoyments. Now, Augustinian theologies of this sort regularly yield a potentially tormenting existential problem concerning the authenticity of spiritual experience. I have, perhaps, undergone a profound experience of conversion and transformation; but can I be sure that it is really the very presence of God's Holy Spirit that I have experienced? And can I be sure that I truly love God *for his own sake* and am not merely using him as a source of elevated pleasures and a more satisfying self-image?

In this latter case, of course, since the true God *cannot* be "used," I would not be relating to God at all, but to a construct projected out of my own perverse heart. Even if I have genuinely experienced God's grace, the moment that I begin to regard grace as something that I can use, something that props up my ego, I have lost touch with the real God and substituted an idol of my own making. The problem of the "pure love of God" and the problem of identifying and turning to the real God turn out to be the same problem, since the real God simply *is* the transcendent one who cannot be manipulated for any human purposes and so can only be "enjoyed" for his own sake.

This is not an insight original with Luther; the problem was widely recognized in medieval Western theology, especially by monastic and spiritual writers whose theologizing took place in close proximity to pastoral care and spiritual direction. Luther was intensely aware of these traditional dialectics, and he works them out with great care and vigor in, for example, the *Lectures on Romans* (1515-1516).

Best known is his depiction of the sinner as *incurvatus in se,* "curved in on self":

our nature, by the corruption of the first sin, is so deeply curved in on itself that it not only bends the best gifts of God toward itself and enjoys them (as is plain in the works-righteous and hypocrites), or rather even uses God himself in order to attain these gifts, but it also fails to realize that it so wickedly, curvedly, and viciously seeks all things, even God, for its own sake. (*WA* 56:304)

What is perhaps not so widely noticed is that Luther's account of the cunning of self-love is closely related to the analysis of idolatry set forth in his comments on Romans 1:19-20. According to Luther, idolatry arises when the concept of deity, which is known to all human beings, is referred to the wrong object; idolatry is a willful mistake in completing what Luther calls the *theological-practical syllogism,* whose form is something like this:

Major: There is some such reality as deity, which is mighty, immortal, invisible, just, good, and to be adored.

Minor: X is the true possessor of this deity.

Conclusion: X is the one whom we shall adore.

Idolatry arises when human beings specify *X* willfully, according to their own wishes and desires. *Crude* idolatry ascribes deity to Jupiter or some other such fictive entity, but there is a much more insidious *spiritual* idolatry that remains a problem, perhaps *the* problem, within the church, as Luther writes:

By the same steps people even today arrive at a spiritual and more subtle idolatry, which is now quite common, by which God is worshiped, not as he is, but as he is imagined and reckoned to be. For ingratitude and love of vanity (that is, one's sense of oneself and of one's own righteousness or, as they say, one's good intention) violently blind people, so that they are incorrigible, and unable to believe otherwise than that they are acting splendidly and pleasing God. And in this way they form a God favorable to themselves, even though he really is not so. And so they more truly worship their fantasy than the true God, whom they believe to be like that fantasy. (*WA* 56:179)

In other words, idolatry constructs the syllogism in some such fashion as this:

Major: There is some such reality as deity, which is mighty, immortal, invisible, just, good, and to be adored.

Minor: The one who gives me pleasurable spiritual experiences and a better self-image is the true possessor of deity.

Conclusion: The one who gives me pleasurable spiritual experiences and a better self-image is the one whom I shall adore.

This is as much as to say, "God is one whom I can use to my own spiritual advantage," and such a God is as much a fiction as Jupiter. The problem, then, is that the X must be specified in such a way as to resist the subtle machinations of spiritual idolatry, to make it clear that the One to whom the church ascribes deity can in no way be manipulated to serve the wishes and desires of the corrupted self. And this is a problem that theology can only address by examining the specific contours of God's own self-revelation and self-giving.

V

Luther's first strategy for addressing this problem, developed in the years from the *Lectures on Romans* to the indulgence controversy, was the so-called *theology of the cross*. Protestants today tend to use the phrase "theology of the cross" to refer to anything in theology that they like, and so I need to stress that I am using the term in a limited, technical sense to refer to a very specific theological strategy typical of Luther's thought in the period leading up to the controversy on indulgences.

In the theology of the cross, using the term in this technical sense, Luther addresses the problem of idolatrous self-seeking with what might be called a *strategy of contrariety*. It is a very specific, very simple, and quite perversely brilliant theological move. How can we tell that we are really clinging to God and not to an idol of our own self-seeking? Luther answers that the gracious presence of the true God is so excruciatingly painful and distastefully unpalatable to our nature that we can have no imaginable self-interested motivation for enduring it.

Therefore the excellent God, after he has justified and given his spiritual gifts, lest that ungodly nature rush upon them to enjoy them (for they are very lovely and powerfully incite to enjoyment), immediately brings tribulation, exercises, and examines, lest the person perish eternally by such ignorance. For thus a person learns to love and worship God purely, when one worships God not for the sake of his grace and gifts, but for himself alone. (*WA* 56:305)

Luther presses this point to the limit, arguing that in some persons, self-regarding love can only be overcome if grace comes in the form of actual damnation: only when the soul resigns itself to hell for the sake of God has it come to love God for his own sake:

> But it is asked whether God has ever willed or wills that persons resign themselves to hell and hand themselves over to damnation or to the anathema from Christ for the sake of his will. I answer that this has happened in many cases, and especially in those who are imperfect in charity or the pure love of God. For the love of concupiscence, which is so deeply implanted in them, must be dug out. But it is not dug out except through a superabundant infusion of grace or through this most harsh resignation [i.e., to damnation]. For "nothing soiled will enter into the kingdom of God" (Rev. 21:27). But now no persons know whether they love God purely unless they experience in themselves that they would even desire not to be saved and would not refuse to be damned if it were pleasing to God. (*WA* 56:391)

We misunderstand this early theology of the cross if we don't see that it is a strikingly simple response to a very specific problem. The problem is that we don't want to come into God's presence for God's sake, but for the sake of all the good things he can do for us: we want to *use* God. Luther answers: If it's really God, then he will crucify and torture you, and thus leave you no reason to cling to him except for his own sweet sake.

This strategy of contrariety is related to an ambiguity in Luther's Christology that becomes unmistakable in the years 1516-1517. How is Christ's role as Savior to be conceived? Is salvation a matter of replicating a *pattern* displayed in Christ, or of communion with his *person*, sharing in what is his and in what he is? Both ways of thinking are present in Luther's thought from the beginning, and the motif of the "happy exchange" certainly presses toward an understanding of salvation as communion with Christ's person.

The *Lectures on Romans* are not altogether consistent on this point. The communion soteriology is certainly present: "But if he made his righteousness mine, now I am righteous with the same righteousness by which he is righteous" (*WA* 56:204). But especially in the latter part of the lectures, much of Luther's rhetorical passion appears to be invested in an *exemplarist* Christology for which Christ as Savior is the productive archetype of a pattern of experience which is repeated in those who believe:

> For Christ too was damned and forsaken more than all the saints, nor was his suffering easy, as some imagine. But he really and truly offered himself to God the Father for us unto eternal damnation. And his human nature was in no other condition than that of a human being eternally damned to hell. On account of his love for God, God immediately raised him from death and hell and so devoured hell. It is necessary that all his saints imitate this, some less, some more; the more perfect they are in love, the more meekly and easily they can do this. But Christ did this in the harshest way of all. (*WA* 56:392)

The theology of the cross naturally presses in this direction: Christ is the one in whom it is revealed that God kills in order to give life, casts down to hell in order to exalt to heaven. And as Luther develops the theology of the cross in 1516-1518, the tension between exemplarist soteriology and communion soteriology becomes more and more marked. A good example is the ambiguity of the notion of "sufferings and the cross" in the *Heidelberg Disputation,* the last and most impressive statement of this transitional *theologia crucis,* written as Luther's thinking was already beginning to move in new directions.

Thus Luther writes in his exposition of the twentieth thesis:

> For because human beings have abused the knowledge of God from works, God willed in turn to be known in sufferings, and to rebuke that wisdom of invisible things by the wisdom of visible things, so that in this way those who did not worship God manifest from works might worship him hidden in sufferings. (*Studienausgabe* I:208)

It is just not clear here whether Luther is saying that God is known hiddenly in the *particular* sufferings of Christ on Calvary, or in the phenomenon of suffering in general. The suspicion that the exemplarist reading might well be the best is strengthened by the explanation of thesis 21:

> It is clear that since [the theologian of glory] does not know Christ, he does not know God hidden in sufferings. Therefore he prefers works to

sufferings, and glory to the cross, power to weakness, wisdom to folly and, in general, good to evil. . . . But God is not to be found except in sufferings and the cross, as has already been said. Therefore the friends of the cross say that the cross is good and works are evil, since through the cross works are destroyed and Adam is crucified, who is rather built up by works. (*Studienausgabe* I:208-9)

Here it does seem that knowing God in Christ means discerning the *pattern* of God's contrary working as manifested in Christ; the theologian of the cross has learned from the figure of Christ the principle that God's saving grace comes to us under the form of its opposite. This exemplarism is, to be sure, never Luther's only soteriological language; the issue is simply unresolved in his early work, with the exemplarism predominant in contexts controlled by the strategy of contrariety.

It should be clear that this strategy utterly excludes the sort of confident assurance of God's favor that Luther later came to teach; on the contrary, for the early *theologia crucis* our *uncertainty* of salvation plays an important role in weaning us from self-interested piety: we must learn to cling to God even though it seems most likely that he will damn us.

It has therefore sometimes been assumed that this theology, and the piety of humble submission to spiritual suffering that accompanies it, must have been so crushingly self-tormenting that it only added fuel to Luther's spiritual agony and his quest for a gracious God. But there is little warrant for this in the texts; on the contrary, Luther seems to have found it a comforting doctrine. Even though it forbids the undialectical confidence in God's mercy that Luther later came to teach, it nonetheless allows the sinner yearning for God under the cross a sort of paradoxical assurance, a sense of being at least in the appropriate place before God, which sustains the heart and enables it to endure to the end. In a sort of "trusting despair," *fiducialis desperatio,* the sinner afflicted by grace discerns in her afflictions the saving hand of God, whose redemptive love secures itself from abuse by hiding under its apparent opposite. There is no real evidence that Luther regarded this consolation as inadequate; the impetus to reshape his thought in a new configuration came from the theological tradition, not from the anxious yearnings of a troubled conscience.

VI

It is quite crucial to realize that Luther did *not* initially criticize indulgences for being legalistic, or worry that they would trouble consciences by forcing people to rely on their own works for salvation. On the contrary, his pastoral worry about the indulgence sales was that simple people were being misled into confusing the external remission of penalties with the crucifying inner grace which drives out self-seeking. Thus he writes:

> And so let us diligently take care lest indulgences . . . become for us a cause of security and indolence and loss of interior grace. But let us take action carefully in order that the sickness of our nature may be perfectly healed and we thirst to come to God out of love for him and hatred of this life and disgust with ourselves, that is, let us assiduously seek his healing grace. (*WABr* 12:9)

The problem with indulgences was therefore that they offered a cheap and easy way of avoiding the pain of authentic inward transformation.

It is during the following year, between the summer and fall of 1517 and the summer and fall of 1518, in the midst of the great controversy in which Luther soon found himself embroiled, that most scholars now see a crucial turn in his thinking. By the end of 1518, the theme of humble endurance of God's crucifying grace is receding into the background, not repudiated, but no longer the focal point. The new center of Luther's theology of grace is now the heart's confident assurance of the promised mercy of God in Christ, what he will later describe simply as "the faith which grasps Christ," *fides apprehensiva Christi.*

On one level, then, there is no mystery about what happened in 1518: Luther came to define faith as confident assurance of God's forgiveness. What is not so obvious and needs investigation are the grounds and significance of this conviction: how did Luther get to that point and what does this imply about the direction of his thinking as a whole?

We can get a more concrete sense of Luther's new position from the memorandum that he presented to Cardinal Cajetan during their October meetings in Augsburg. Cajetan had challenged Luther's insistence that those who come to the sacrament of penance are to believe confidently that they receive God's grace and forgiveness thereby; Luther's main defense of his position appeals to Christ's words in Matthew 16:19:

> It is necessary, under peril of eternal damnation and the sin of unbelief, to believe these words of Christ: Whatever you loose on earth will be loosed also in heaven. Therefore if you come forward to the sacrament of penance and do not believe firmly that you are absolved in heaven, you come forward to judgment and damnation, because you do not believe that Christ has spoken what is true: Whatever you loose, etc., and so by your doubt you make Christ a liar, which is a horrible sin. . . . But when you believe the word of Christ, you honor his word and by this work you are righteous, etc. (*WA* 2:13-14)

This makes pretty unmistakably clear, I think, the most important thing that happened to Luther in 1518: he has rethought his theology of grace in the context of the theology of the *sacraments*. This is indeed new; Luther seems to have paid no serious attention at all to sacramental theology until he got embroiled in the indulgence controversy. But in that controversy, his emphasis on the inner purification of the heart by grace was bound to raise the question: "What *do* you think the sacrament is good for, anyway?" Luther seems to have anticipated this: as early as the summer of 1517, when he was already disturbed by the indulgence sales but had not yet made his formal public statement, we find him for the first time taking up sacramental issues in earnest in his lectures.

The problem in sacramental theology that proved crucial for Luther was that of the relationship between the outward sacramental action, the grace of God, and the faith required of the participant in the sacrament. The story of Luther's struggles with this question, from the summer of 1517 to the summer of 1518, is much too complicated to rehearse here: in the spring of 1518 alone, Luther not only thought up but actually published three different and mutually exclusive solutions to the problem, including one that is almost indistinguishable from the view later associated with Zwingli.

What finally emerged, in the summer of 1518, from this frantic rethinking — recall that Luther was trying to work through the theological issue while at the same time explaining to the world why he shouldn't be burned at the stake for heresy — seems to have been shaped primarily by reflection on texts such as Matthew 16:19: "Whatever you loose on earth is loosed in heaven." To the question "What is the sacrament good for, anyway?" Luther finally responds: the concrete, external, public sacramental act in the church is the concrete, external, public act of Jesus Christ in the church. When we come to the sacrament, we run into Jesus Christ: his word, his act, his authority. The question with which every participant in the sacraments is confronted, therefore, is simply this: Is Jesus Christ telling the truth here? Can he do what he promises? Can we count on what he says?

The new focus of his thought on this sacramental situation is what makes all the difference; this is what gives Luther's theology after 1518 a very different shape from his early thought, even though he continued to be concerned with many of the same issues. Where the critical point in his earlier theology of grace is God's crucifying contradiction of sinful human nature, here the point on which everything hinges is the authority of Christ the Savior, exercised concretely in the sacramental signs in the church.

Faith is now sharply defined by this sacramental situation: faith is openness to and acknowledgment of Christ's authority in its concrete sacramental exercise. There is no other prerequisite than such faith for the fruitful reception of the sacrament, because the sacrament is itself the public act in which Christ bestows his grace on the ungodly. The public sacramental life of the church is now seen as the *locus* of assurance, of certitude, the place where an entirely undialectical saving communication takes place.

VII

The insight that sacramental theology was the hinge for the "turn" in Luther's thinking in 1518 is by no means original with me; the point is widely acknowledged in the scholarly literature. But I want to go on and claim that this turn is described quite wrongly if we take it as a "Reformation turn" *away from* the catholic tradition, the founding of a new Christianity. On the contrary, I would argue that this turn was a turn *toward* the very heart of the catholic tradition.

To understand the broader implications of what happened in Luther's thinking in 1518, we must return to the theme of idolatry. One helpful way of describing the implications of the "turn" we have been considering is as a change in the primary way in which Luther specifies X in the minor premise of this theological-practical syllogism. In the so-called theology of the cross, this was governed by what we have called the strategy of contrariety: the X who possesses divinity is the one who crucifies me. By determinedly making the crucifixion of Jesus the exemplar and paradigm of all God's gracious dealings with fallen humanity, the way is closed to the spiritual idolatry that covertly identifies God as the source of spiritual goods that prop up the self. This leads, as we saw, to a dialectical, paradoxical account of faith: the one whom I am to adore and in whom I am to put my trust is precisely the one whom all experience says is bent on destroying me.

The net effect of Luther's new focus on the authority of Christ in the sacramental sign is to subordinate this strategy of contrariety to a *strategy of particularity*, well summarized in a line from one of Luther's later sermons on John 3: "We have a definite Lord, one we can grasp" (*WA* 47:203). From 1518 on, Luther's primary identification of the X in the minor of the theological-practical syllogism will be: "The true possessor of deity is *the one whom I encounter here* — in the particular flesh of Jesus Christ and in the concrete sacramental sign." It is the particularity and concreteness of God's presence that now bear the brunt of the task of foreclosing idolatry; the true God, who by definition cannot be used, is the God who makes himself available as he chooses, here and not there, in the flesh born of Mary and the specificity of his church's sacramental practice, not in the groves and high places consecrated by our religious speculation and self-interest.

Thus, for example, in his 1537 exposition of John 14, Luther begins by describing idolatry in his usual terms:

> But human reason acts in this way: when it hears the name of God and that it should trust in him, it is so stupid that it rushes in at once and wants to set up according to its own mind and thoughts the ways and rules of how one should deal with God. (*WA* 45:481)

This idolatrous willfulness of reason, Luther goes on to say, is countered only when faith is presented with an unmistakably *particular* object:

> Since the terms "trusting God" and "serving God" must suffer being stretched to such lengths that everyone draws them out to fit his own ideas, one interpreting them one way, another in another way — therefore God has placed himself and fixed himself at a definite place and a definite person where he wants to be found and encountered, so that one may not go astray. Now this is none other than the person of Christ himself, in whom the whole fullness of deity dwells bodily. . . . Therefore Christ wants to say: "You have heard that you are to trust God; but I

want also to show you where you will genuinely meet him, so that you don't make yourselves an idol according to your own ideas under his name. This means: If you want to believe in God, then believe in me. If you want to orient your faith and trust rightly, that they may not be out of place or false, then orient them to me, for in me the entire deity is and dwells in fullness." (*WA* 45:481)

In this new configuration, faith is no longer ineluctably involved in a never-ending dialectic of trust and despair; it is the altogether nondialectical confidence that acknowledges the unambiguous authority of the saving Christ concretely present in his church. A shift thus takes place in the primary sense of the notion of God's hiddenness: in Luther's early "theology of the cross," God hides his saving presence in the torment he visits on his elect; in the mature theology, the gracious hiddenness of God is primarily a matter of his *lowliness,* his *kenosis* in the incarnate Son, in his chosen signs, and in his saints. The tribulations of the faithful are no longer *identical* with the grace that saves them, although they drive them to seek that grace and are the veil under which it is hidden from the proud and mighty of this world. The saving presence of God is not in itself dialectical or ambiguous in the least, although high-flying religiosity must humble itself to find it.

The role of this particularity in closing off the broad way of idolatry clarifies an important point about Luther's "turn" that has too seldom been noticed: the need to comfort the anxious conscience was *not* its primary motivation. As we have seen, Luther's overriding pastoral concern throughout the indulgence controversy was that ordinary people were being misled about where and how grace is to be found. Initially, this concern took the form, prescribed by the strategy of contrariety, of a worry that people were being provided with a cheap strategy for avoiding the rigors of inner transformation under the cross; his aim was to disturb rather than to console the conscience.

Luther never abandoned that concern, but as he wrestled with sacramental theology against the background of the question of the true God and the true mode of his presence, he began to define the primary issue differently. The real question with which I am confronted when I approach the sacrament of penance is whether I believe that Christ speaks the truth when he says that whatever the church shall loose on earth will be loosed in heaven. If I believe that he does speak the truth, then I am

28

called to put all my trust in his authority to save — and that means that I confess that Christ is the true God. The sacraments thus hold out Christ and say, "Behold your God!"

If the one who authorizes the absolution of my sins is the true God, then indeed I may have an entirely undialectical assurance of salvation; this answer to the pastoral problem of the troubled conscience was a deeply important practical by-product of Luther's new appreciation of the sacraments. But that assurance of faith is at the same time, first and foremost, *true worship*, the acknowledgment of God in his Godhead, obedience and submission of the heart. Anxiety about my unworthiness and presumption on my merits are alike failures to acknowledge the authority of God in his concrete saving presence. As Jared Wicks has pointed out, this motif became even more prominent in Luther's later struggles against the Swiss and the Baptists, but it was already present at the very heart of the developments of 1518.

It is in this perspective that I would argue that Luther's development in 1518 might best be described as a turn toward rather than away from the heart of the catholic tradition. Protestant Luther scholars have often said that Luther broke with the dogmatism, sacramentalism, and mysticism of the catholic tradition; I want to turn this around and argue that the 1518 "turn" anchored Luther more deeply than ever before in the traditions of catholic dogma, catholic sacramentalism, and catholic mysticism.

Luther's theology was a "mystical" theology from the start, in the precise sense that it was a theology focused on the transformation of human persons by union with God in the sheer transcendence and otherness of his Godhead. But looking at Luther's development up to 1518, we might not be convinced that this mysticism was evolving in a genuinely catholic direction. Theologies intensely concerned with inner transformation and the purifying presence of God have, after all, been known to become unmoored from the catholic tradition, and while one would not want to say that this had happened to the Luther of 1516 or 1517, one might wonder where this radical Augustinian theology of uncreated grace was going.

Thus one might be concerned that Luther's comparative disinterest in the sacraments, innocent enough in his early lectures on the Psalms, is growing somewhat ominous in the *Lectures on Romans,* especially in the context of his single-minded focus on the inner life. It is, surely, a bit strange for a theologian to expound Romans 6 without ever talking about the sacrament of baptism!

Likewise, the committed Christocentricity of the author of the *Lectures* is certainly not in question, no more than his formal Christological orthodoxy, but here, too, we might wonder whether this particular Christocentrism really *needs* the Christological dogma in order to function. Had Luther continued to develop his Christology along the lines of the *theologia crucis*, the outcome might well have been very much at right angles to the Chalcedonian tradition, whether or not it ever burst the exoskeleton of traditional orthodoxy. Might one not even suspect that the Christocentricity of the "theology of the cross" was threatened with subversion by a kind of unitarianism of the Holy Spirit, for which Christ would finally be only the productive archetype in which the dynamic pattern of the Spirit's transforming grace is displayed? Would such an exemplarist soteriology really need to confess Christ as a divine person who has assumed true human flesh?

In all these respects, the "turn" initiated in 1518 was a turn toward the core of the catholic tradition, a reaffirmation of its dogmatic and sacramental heart. For Luther after 1518, Christ is central not as pattern but as person; we are saved by the faith that acknowledges his authority, competence, and willingness to rescue those who call on him. The gospel that is proclaimed and sacramentally enacted in the church is a word that calls us to put all our trust in this particular person, Jesus the Son of Mary; thus who Jesus Christ is and where he gets the authority to promise such astounding things become the central theological questions. Or as Luther put it in his lectures on Psalm 2 from the beginning of the 1530s, what is constitutive of the gospel is the identity of the one to whom it points:

> This is to be a new doctrine. The old doctrine is this: Believe in God. . . .
> The law urges us to our works; that is the highest thing in Moses. But·
> here no law is proposed, there is no exaction but a casting down, what
> is set before us is not our works but the Son of God. It offers us an object,
> which we ourselves are not, but rather: "My Son." The definite doctrine
> that this King and teacher Christ is to urge and exercise is this: not to
> teach the law or our works, but Christ, the Son of God, that one may
> look to him. . . . Therefore the chief doctrine, and the sum of all that
> surpasses Moses, is not to hear the law, what I should do, but to hear
> *who that one is. (WA* 40/2:249; emphasis added)

The Christological dogma, and with it the doctrine of the Trinity, are for just this reason much more clearly constitutive for Luther's theology of grace after 1518 than in the *Lectures on Romans* or the *Heidelberg Disputation*. Indeed, Luther can quite straightforwardly identify the doctrine of justification with the Christological dogma of the ancient church, as he does in his *Sermons on John 6:*

> You have heard already that he calls himself "the Son of Man." In this way he wants to show that he has our true flesh and blood, which he took to himself from the Virgin Mary, in which eternal life are to be found. *This is the article of justification:* the Holy Spirit wills that one under no circumstances learn, known, imagine, hear, or accept another God besides this God whose flesh and blood we imprint and grasp in our hearts if we want to be saved. We are not to let ourselves be taught a God who sits up above in heaven in his throne room, who is therefore to be sought only in the divinity. For thus you will be led astray; but if you want to escape death and to be saved, let no God come to you besides the Son of Man. In his flesh and blood you will find God; that is where he has located himself, there you will meet him, where the Son of Man is. (*WA* 23:201; emphasis added)

The same holds true of catholic sacramentalism. After 1518, Luther is quite clear that it is *in and through* the public performance of the sacramental signs in the visible church that grace is bestowed on those who believe. His mystical theology of uncreated grace, the purifying encounter with God in his very Godhead, is henceforth anchored to the preaching and ritual of the church as the concrete *loci* of God's certain, undialectical presence. Indeed, it becomes an explicit theological axiom for Luther that inward and spiritual grace is given *only* in and through the public, bodily, sacramental practice of the church. This principled sacramentalism was immediately given with the 1518 "turn," although, of course, it becomes even more pronounced and explicit in the controversies with the Radical Reformation and the Swiss. As Luther put it in 1525:

> Now that God has let his holy gospel go forth, he deals with us in two ways: on the one hand, outwardly, on the other hand, inwardly. Outwardly he deals with us through the oral word of the gospel and through bodily signs, such as baptism and the sacrament. Inwardly he deals with us through the Holy Spirit and faith along with other gifts. But all this in such measure and in such order that the outward elements should and must come first. And the inward things come afterwards and by

means of the outward, for he has decided to give the inward element to no one except by means of the outward element. For he will give no one the Spirit or faith without the outward word and sign which he has instituted. (*WA* 18:136)

Luther's impatient arguments for the reform of sacramental practice and theology and his frequent vilification of received usages and opinions should not therefore be allowed to obscure what might be called his "deep catholic" commitment to the sacramentality of grace, with its unmistakable patristic resonances: for Luther and the Fathers alike, the worship of the *ekklesia* is the mystical epiphany of God's *philanthropia* in Christ. It is no accident at all that Luther's major work of 1519 was a series of sermons describing the way in which Christian existence is founded and formed by the sacraments.

Does this dogmatic sacramentalism remain a mystical theology? A full answer to this would require a careful untangling of the complexities of Luther's developed theology of justification, of the relationships of such notions as word and presence, imputation and union. It is a deeply engrained assumption of a certain kind of modern Luther scholarship that Luther's later emphasis on the external word and the humanity of Christ is incompatible with such mystical notions of saving union with God in his very transcendent deity. I would argue, however, that this assumption does not survive careful reading of the texts; Luther's point is rather that the sacramental word and the humanity of Christ are precisely the concrete points of encounter at which we are united with God in his deity.

Two passages from works of Luther's maturity may serve to illustrate this. The first is from Luther's 1531 *Sermons on John 6:*

Many teachers have taught in this way, and I too in time past was that sort of doctor, so that I excluded the humanity and thought that I did well if I divided the divinity and humanity of Christ from one another. In time past the very most exalted theologians did this, so that they fled from the humanity of Christ to his divinity and clung to the latter, and thought that one did not need to know the humanity of Christ. But one must mount up to the divinity of Christ, and cling to it, in such a way that one does not leave behind the humanity of Christ and come to the divinity of Christ by itself. Otherwise we fall down from the ladder, in the name of all the devils! . . . If you can humble yourself, cling to the word with your heart, and stand by the humanity of Christ, *then you will find the Godhead,* and the Father and the Holy Spirit, and *the entire Godhead will take hold of you. (WA* 33:155-56; emphasis added)

The second passage is from the *Lectures on Genesis,* which occupied Luther's teaching for the last decade of his life. Luther is expounding Genesis 28:17; his argument is that the "house of God" and "gate of heaven" are present concretely here on earth, in the earthly church in which the word and the sacraments are celebrated: "Direct your steps to the place where the word sounds forth and the sacraments are administered, and there inscribe the title *THE GATE OF GOD*" (*WA* 43:599). Thus God is to be found at concrete places here on earth. But far from thinking that we should therefore renounce the aim of union with God in his deity, Luther insists that it is precisely in this sacramental and ecclesial concreteness that we are united to God:

> Thus the church is established among human beings when there comes about a dwelling-together of God with human beings, to this end, that it may be the gate of heaven and that we may go forth from this earthly life into the eternal and heavenly life. Who can marvel enough at this or comprehend it, that God dwells with humans? *This indeed is that heavenly Jerusalem which comes down out of heaven from God and has the splendor of God,* as the *Apocalypse* says (21:2). And this is a definition which gets to the essence: "The church is the place or the people where God dwells, in order to bring us to enter the kingdom of heaven, for it is heaven's gate." (*WA* 43:601)

VIII

As I mentioned at the start of this essay, this reading of Luther's development suggests that the Western schism, far from being the appropriate historical outcome of principled theological disagreement, was instead a tragic chapter of accidents. In particular, there are no historical grounds for believing that the schism was the necessary outcome of Luther's theology of grace. On the contrary, on the one occasion when Luther's theological proposals received a somewhat careful hearing from a representative of the Roman Church, at his meetings with Cardinal Cajetan in Augsburg in 1518, the conclusion reached was that his doctrine of justifying faith was *not* obviously heretical or in clear opposition to the tradition of the church.

While Cajetan only understood Luther's views imperfectly and regarded them as temerarious and mistaken, he was ready to recommend that they receive further discussion and consideration before a final judgment was reached.

Schism was not the necessary consequence of Luther's theological vision but the contingent outcome of the badly managed *causa Lutheri*, the ecclesiastical examination of Luther's orthodoxy in 1518-1519, and the controversy over teaching authority with which it became entangled. On Luther's side, the final break with the church authorities came in the wake of Leo X's bull of November 1518; in that document, as Luther saw it, Leo arrogated to himself the power of defining church teaching without accountability to Scripture, the Fathers, or the ancient canons. This led him to conclude that the Roman Church was irrevocably committed to the claim that the authority of the pope stood even above Holy Scripture, and it was in this context that Luther came, over the next several years, to believe that the papacy was the prophesied Antichrist of the last days, a conviction he held to his dying day with a literalistic fervor that his modern interpreters have rarely been willing to take as seriously as he did.

When Luther became convinced that the papacy was Antichrist, all the energy of his theological vision was harnessed to the forces already working to dissolve the church's unity; this more than anything else made schism inevitable. There is blame enough to go around for this tragic and pointless outcome. The theological obtuseness of the Roman court theologians (Cajetan partly excepted), the inability or unwillingness of the Roman authorities to appropriate their own best ecclesiological traditions, and the unlovely influence of financial politics on the handling of the doctrinal issues all played a considerable role, as did Luther's impatience and anger, his inability to take stupid and inappropriate papal teaching in stride at all calmly (perhaps because his own early view of the papal office was unrealistically high), as well as his tendency to dramatize his own situation in apocalyptic terms. The tragedy is compounded, moreover, on the reading that I have proposed, by the irony of the fact that in material theological terms the Luther of 1519 arguably did greater justice to the core convictions of the catholic tradition than the Luther of 1517.

The Reform of the Mass:
Evangelical, but Still Catholic

Frank C. Senn

THE SOURCE and summit of religious devotion in medieval Western Europe was the order of worship in word and sacrament called *Missa* — "the Mass." The sixteenth-century Reformers were right in saying that "the mass dominated everything." The mass sanctified life, space, and time. The occasional sacramental services of baptism, confirmation, ordination, marriage, and burial were celebrated in the context of the mass. Penance served the purpose of communion discipline. The visitation of the sick included the extended distribution of Holy Communion. Pilgrimages culminated with the celebration of a mass at the place of pilgrimage. The church year, with its seasons and special days, provided "proper" material for the celebration of each mass.

The order of the mass had not changed much since the ancient church. As it evolved during the Middle Ages it acquired a preparatory office conducted in the sacristy or at the foot of the altar that included a prayer of forgiveness and pardon. The mass proper included an entrance rite: Introit and Gloria Patri, Kyrie, Gloria in excelsis; a liturgy of the word: salutation and collect, Epistle reading, Gradual with alleluia or tract, Gospel reading, sermon, Nicene Creed; a liturgy of the sacrament: offertory antiphon and prayers, the great thanksgiving (proper preface, Sanctus, and Canon), the Our Father with embolism ("Deliver us . . . from every evil . . ."), fraction and commingling, Agnus Dei, communion with devotional prayers and communion antiphon; and a dismissal rite: post-communion collect, dismissal, and benediction. During the course of the millennium between the classical Roman sacramentaries and the sixteenth-century Reformation a few ancient items fell out of use and other items, stemming from Gallican spirituality, were added.[1] But the style of celebration of the mass changed considerably. The Reformation's critique of the mass had more to do with the way the mass was celebrated and the practices associated with it than with its order and content. With regard to changes needed in order and content, the Reformers could appeal to the plethora of mass-books in different provinces with their numerous textual and rubrical variations.

The Celebration of Mass in the Middle Ages

The order of worship called *Missa* (the name is derived from the untranslatable concluding text — *Ite missa est*) had been called *Leitourgia* ("the work of the people") in the patristic period. By the late Middle Ages, however, the Western Catholic mass had ceased to be understood as a "liturgy" or work of the people. The people's role in the mass had been diminished in several ways. The retention of ecclesiastical Latin as the language of the mass rather than the development of vernacular languages, such as the Greek missionary brothers Cyril and Methodius had done when they translated the Bible and the Byzantine liturgy into Slavonic, reduced popular participation — although Latin was widely used in Western European courts and universities, and even illiterate people were taught the basic Latin responses. Sometimes choirs took over the people's roles and sang the canticles, the Creed, and the responses. The offertory and eucharistic prayers (the "Canon of the Mass") were recited silently by the priest and were not heard by the people. Often masses were celebrated "privately" for special intentions. Votive masses were offered for some benefit for the living or the dead, but usually for the repose of the souls in purgatory. People paid to have these masses celebrated, and by the late Middle Ages a veritable

---

1. Among ancient elements in the liturgy that fell out of use during the Middle Ages were the Old Testament lesson, the responsorial psalm, and litanized intercessory prayers. On the other hand, private prayers said by the celebrant multiplied in the preparatory office *(Confiteor)*, at the offertory *(Secreta)*, and during communion. For the most definitive and thorough study of the history of the mass see Joseph A. Jungmann, *The Mass of the Roman Rite: Its Origins and Development*, trans. Francis A. Brunner (Westminster, Md.: Christian Classics, 1986), especially vol. 1, pp. 44ff.

proletariat of "mass-priests" or "altarists" had arisen who did no other pastoral work. These "private masses" were "said" by a priest, attended by one or two assistants. Often a number of masses were celebrated simultaneously in medieval church buildings, which were divided into numerous compartments called side chapels. The theory of the limited value of each mass contributed to the multiplication of masses.[2]

Perhaps most grievously, regular preaching on the readings during the mass had ceased, and people were no longer receiving communion. People had become spectators rather than participants, and to the extent that teaching was given to the people it tended to be allegorical fables and allegorical interpretations of the complicated ceremonies of the mass that turned the mass into a dramatic reenactment of Calvary.[3] But the benefits of Christ's atoning sacrifice on Calvary were obscured since the people no longer regularly received the sacrament of the body and blood of Christ at mass. Indeed, the very essence of mass devotion was gazing at the host, which was elevated by the priest during the words of institution in the Canon (which was recited silently by the priest while the choir continued to sing the *Sanctus* and *Benedictus qui venit*). This dramatic high point of the mass, fostered by the consecration theology attending the dogma of transubstantiation, was signaled by the ringing of the "Sanctus bells" as everyone genuflected. So sacrosanct had the consecrated elements become that the laity could not touch them or even receive communion from the chalice for fear that the precious blood of Christ might be spilled.

By the fifteenth century there was widespread recognition that the mass, like other aspects of church life, needed reform. Among his wide-ranging proposals for reform, the German Cardinal Nicholas of Cusa called in mass-books in his diocese to correct them according to an archetype and promoted conciliar legislation to curb abuses.[4] He repeatedly denounced the extravagant promises attached to the celebration of mass on the grounds

---

2. For a thorough background on abuses in praxis in the medieval celebration of the mass see John Jay Hughes, *Stewards of the Lord: A Reappraisal of Anglican Orders* (London and Sydney: Sheed and Ward, 1970).

3. Ferdinand Pratzner, in *Messe und Kreuzesopfer. Die Krise der Sakramentalen Idee bei Luther und in der Mittelalterlichen Scholastik* (Wien: Herder, 1970), discusses the impact of an affective understanding of *repraesentatio* on the medieval view of the eucharistic sacrifice.

4. See John P. Dolan, *History of the Reformation*, intro. by Jaroslav Pelikan (New York and Toronto: Mentor-Omega, 1965), pp. 139ff.

that they were misleading people into a form of "Judaism" and promoting superstition. But he ultimately failed, as did others. It was Martin Luther who first successfully launched a movement for the total reform of the Catholic Church of the West.

Luther's Liturgical Reforms

Martin Luther laid the foundations for liturgical reform as well as for other aspects of the Reformation. In *The Babylonian Captivity of the Church* (1520)[5] he attacked the heart of medieval religion: the sacramental system. He denied that there were seven sacraments and "for the moment" accepted only "baptism, penance, and the bread." He asserted that the sacrament of the bread was held captive in three ways: the cup was withheld from lay communicants, the mystery of the eucharist was rationalized with the dogma of transubstantiation, and the mass was offered as "a good work and a sacrifice" *(opus bonum et sacrificium)* instead of being received as the gift of Christ to his church.

This third "captivity" comprehends two related but separate issues: the mass is not a good work and the mass is not a sacrifice.[6] The use of the mass in the service of works righteousness *(Werkgerechtigkeit),* by which the faithful try to gain God's favor without faith in God's promises, could be corrected by preaching and teaching the gospel of justification by faith and by abolishing the "traffic" in masses (i.e., votive masses). But the assault on the mass as a "sacrifice" had liturgical consequences for the *ordo missae* itself since it involved a liturgical reorientation. Luther held that the sacrament is not what the church offers to God (especially the special intentions in votive masses) but the gift of communion, which the faithful receive as "the last will and testament of Christ."

The liturgical consequence of the assault on the mass-sacrifice became clear when Luther undertook a revision of the Latin mass in his treatise on the *Formula Missae et Communiones (Form of the Mass and Communion*

---

5. See *Luther's Works,* vol. 36 (Philadelphia: Fortress Press, 1959), pp. 3ff.

6. Carl F. Wislöff, *The Gift of Communion: Luther's Controversy with Rome on Eucharistic Sacrifice,* trans. Joseph M. Shaw (Minneapolis: Augsburg, 1964), pp. 56ff., makes a compelling case that Luther's attacks against the mass as "work" and against the mass as "sacrifice," while interrelated, need also to be considered separately.

for the Church at Wittenberg, 1523). His intention was not "to abolish the liturgical service of God completely, but rather to purify the one that is now in use from the wretched accretions which corrupt it and to point out an evangelical use."[7] Little departure was made from the medieval mass order until the offertory. "From here on," wrote Luther, "almost everything smacks and savors of sacrifice. And the words of life and salvation [the words of institution] are embedded in the midst of all it, just as the ark of the Lord once stood in the idol's temple next to Dagon. . . . Let us, therefore, repudiate everything that smacks of sacrifice, together with the entire canon, and retain only that which is pure and holy, and so order our mass."[8]

Accordingly, Luther deleted the offertory prayers (the "minor canon") and reduced the *canon missae* to the preface, the words of institution (joined to the preface by a *qui*-clause in the style of a "proper" insertion), and the Sanctus. The purpose of the deletions was to clarify the "direction" of the sacrament as God's gift of communion with Christ rather than the people's offering to God. But Luther also wanted the words of Christ to be proclaimed aloud since they are "a summary of the gospel." So he inserted the *Verba Christi* into the section of the canon that was traditionally sung aloud (the preface), instead of within the post-Sanctus prayers that were customarily recited silently by the priest. Luther's deletion of the Canon may strike us as an extreme measure. We need to remember, however, that the Canon was not the entire eucharistic prayer but only the prayers after the Sanctus, beginning with the *Te igitur.* Few lay worshipers would have noticed the omission of a silent prayer; but they would have noticed the omission of what was, for them, the high point of the mass — the elevation of the host and chalice. By retaining the elevation of the host at the *Benedictus qui venit* ("Blessed is he who comes in the name of the Lord"), Luther managed to retain the most dramatic moment of the medieval mass while effecting the most radical surgery on the Canon.

The most significant reform of the mass, embraced by all the reformers, was that it climaxed in a meal to be shared by the faithful — the Lord's Supper. If there were not communicants to receive the sacrament of the body and blood of Christ, mass would not be celebrated. In the section of the *Formula Missae* dealing with communion practices, Luther encouraged the faithful to receive communion more frequently, recom-

7. *Luther's Works,* vol. 53 (Philadelphia: Fortress Press, 1965), p. 20.
8. *Luther's Works,* vol. 53, p. 26.

mended that the communicants announce their intention to receive the sacrament and submit to a catechetical examination and private confession and absolution, and gather in the chancel for the sacrament where they could make a public testimony.

Even as Luther was revising the Latin liturgy, a number of German liturgies were being published. German masses were being celebrated in monasteries already in 1522. In 1523/1524 Thomas Müntzer published a German mass, Matins, and Vespers with an original plainsong setting for use in Alstedt. An interesting German mass with a revision of the Roman Canon appeared in 1524 in Worms. In the same year German services were introduced in Reutlingen, Wertheim, Königsberg, and Strassburg. The German mass prepared by Diobald Schwartz for Strassburg was an adaptation of the Roman rite.[9] That same year Martin Bucer, who was to have enormous influence on Reformed liturgy, published *Grund und Ursach* with his own proposals for liturgical reform. All of these experiments in vernacular liturgy created a confusing situation, and Luther's friends urged him to provide some guidance. This prompted Luther to prepare his own *German Mass and Order of Service (Deutsche Messe und Gottesdienst,* 1526).[10]

Luther explained in the preface that he had no intentions of changing the *Formula Missae,* which could continue to be sung in towns and universities with trained choirs. But the German mass was "arranged for the sake of the unlearned lay folk" as a kind of "folk mass" *(Lied Messe)* that would serve an educational as well as a liturgical purpose. In this service, which still followed the *ordo missae,* Luther substituted congregational hymns for parts of the mass that had been sung by the choir, specifically the Credo, Sanctus, and Agnus Dei, and indicated that German hymns could be sung in place of the Introit and Gradual as well as during communion. This sparked similar efforts among German Lutherans, and soon metrical hymn versions of the Kyrie, Gloria in excelsis, and other canticles were also composed. The musical elements in the German mass were extensive, since Luther also provided for the chanting of the Collect, Epistle, Gospel, and words of institution. This tradition of a sung liturgy compensated for such

---

9. See William D. Maxwell, *An Outline of Christian Worship: Its Developments and Forms* (London: Oxford University Press, 1936), pp. 88ff. for the order and texts of Schwartz's German mass for Strassburg.

10. *Luther's Works,* vol. 53, pp. 61ff.

didactic elements as the catechetical paraphrase of the Lord's Prayer and the admonition to the communicants. An interesting proposal for the administration of holy communion was that the bread would be distributed immediately after the words over the bread, during which the German Sanctus ("Isaiah, 'twas the prophet who did see") was sung and the host was elevated, and the cup would be distributed immediately after the words over the cup, during which the German Agnus Dei ("O Christ, thou lamb of God") and other songs were sung.

Some have questioned whether Luther intended his German mass to be a definitive order of service since it was his second and final revision of the mass order.[11] The facts that he was adverse to any kind of liturgical legalism (including a legalistic enforcement of his own orders), that he intended his Latin mass to remain in use (especially where trained choirs could sing plainsong or polyphonic settings of the texts), and that he gave his approval to later church orders that did not slavishly follow his own liturgical models (including Saxon church orders that replaced his own) argue against regarding the *Deutsche Messe* as the definitive Lutheran liturgy. But it gave impetus to the flowering of hymnody in the Lutheran Reformation. Luther himself wrote some thirty hymns, encouraged others to write hymns, provided prefaces to several hymnals, and also encouraged the composition of liturgical art music.

Luther's models ensured that the typical Lutheran mass would be a "solemn celebration" (sung throughout, like the Eastern liturgies) with a strong element of adoration and praise. In the elements of adoration and praise Luther found a positive role for the idea of eucharistic sacrifice. In his 1530 *Admonition Concerning the Sacrament,* a work addressed to the laity to promote a "true use" of the sacrament, Luther confessed that "I want to go to the sacrament, not that I would thereby do a good work or achieve merit . . . but to praise and glorify my God who has established it for my reception and out of love and thanks to my Lord and Savior who has instituted it in honor of his suffering in order that I might use it and give thanks for it."[12] While totally distinguishing the sacrament from sacrifice, Luther admitted that there is a true sacrifice of praise and thanksgiving in remembrance of what Christ has done for us and for our salvation. As

11. See Bryan Spinks, *Luther's Liturgical Criteria and His Reform of the Canon of the Mass,* Grove Liturgical Study No. 30 (Bramcote, Notts.: Grove Books, 1982).

12. *Luther's Works,* vol. 38 (Philadelphia: Fortress Press, 1971), pp. 115-16.

a result of such an understanding, Luther believed, "many hymns were included and retained in the mass which deal with thanking and praising [God] in a wonderful and excellent way, as for example, the Gloria in excelsis, the Alleluia, the Patrem [= Creed, not the Lord's Prayer as in the American edition translation], the Preface, the Sanctus, the Benedictus, and the Agnus Dei. In these various parts you find nothing about a sacrifice but only praise and thanks. Therefore, we have also kept them in our mass."[13]

Lutheran Church Orders

Luther's personal influence as the charismatic leader of the Reformation carried great weight, but as the Reformation was officially adopted by princes and city councils for their territories it had to be regulated by church orders *(Kirchenordnungen)*. These documents, which often enlisted the consultative or drafting services of the leading Reformers, addressed matters of church polity, congregational life, charitable institutions, schools, the calendar, and worship, and therefore effected the Protestant "revolution" in social life.[14]

The church orders were legislative documents rather than liturgical books.[15] They presumed the continued use of the pre-Reformation liturgical books and simply provided an *ordo* and gave directions on what should be used or amended in these books. The Sundays, seasons, and major festivals of the church year continued to provide the "propers" for the Lutheran mass, although the number of saints' days was drastically reduced. This arrangement provides exhibit A in the continuity of Reformation mass orders with pre-Reformation mass orders. The first real evangelical liturgical books were the hymnals, which provided songs for the people, and the *cantionales,* which provided music for the choir. These books indicate that the contrasting liturgical styles of Luther's *Formula Missae* and *Deutsche Messe,* with choral singing of the Latin texts and/or congregational singing of vernacular songs, continued to be practiced in Lutheranism (at least until

13. *Luther's Works,* vol. 38, p. 123. Compare with text in *Martin Luthers Werke, Weimar Ausgabe,* vol. 30, part II: 614.30-615.5.

14. See Steven Ozment, *Protestants: The Birth of a Revolution* (New York: Doubleday, 1992), pp. 92-93, 96-103.

15. See the classification of church orders in Luther D. Reed, *The Lutheran Liturgy,* 2nd ed. (Philadelphia: Fortress Press, 1959), pp. 88ff.

the time of J. S. Bach in Leipzig[16]). The Augsburg Confession (1530) testifies to this emerging Lutheran practice in Article XXIV: "Our churches are falsely accused of abolishing the Mass. Actually, the Mass is retained among us and is celebrated with the greatest reverence. Almost all the customary ceremonies are also retained, except that German hymns are interspersed here and there among the parts sung in Latin."[17] Philip Melanchthon elaborates on this in the *Apology of the Augsburg Confession* (1531), Article XXIV: "In our churches the Mass is celebrated every Sunday and on other festivals, when the sacrament is offered to those who wish for it after they have been examined and absolved. We keep traditional liturgical forms, such as the order of the lessons, prayers, vestments, etc."[18]

The positive statements about the celebration of the mass in Lutheran churches in these confessional writings raise the question as to why the mass is treated so negatively in *The Smalcald Articles* (1537), Article II. Here it is said that "The Mass in the papacy must be regarded as the greatest and most horrible abomination because it runs into direct and violent conflict with this fundamental article [on Christ and faith]."[19] We need to clarify that it is not the order or content of the mass that is the issue, but the praxis of the mass: "this dragon's tail — that is, the Mass — has brought forth a brood of vermin and the poison of manifold idolatries." Among the idolatries associated with the mass are requiem and votive masses for the souls in purgatory, the appearance of departed spirits, pilgrimages, mass-fraternities, relics, indulgences, and the invocation of the saints.[20]

Reformed Liturgy

The association of almost every abuse and superstition with the mass makes it remarkable that any semblance of the mass was retained at all by the

16. See Günther Stiller, *Johann Sebastian Bach and Liturgical Life in Leipzig*, ed. Robin A. Leaver, trans. Herbert J. A. Bouman, Daniel F. Poellot, Hilton C. Oswald (St. Louis: Concordia, 1984), esp. Part A: "Liturgical Life in Leipzig in the First Half of the 18th Century."

17. *The Book of Concord*, ed. and trans. Theodore P. Tappert (Philadelphia: Fortress Press, 1959), p. 56.

18. *The Book of Concord*, p. 249.

19. *The Book of Concord*, p. 293.

20. *The Book of Concord*, pp. 295-97.

Reformers. Yet even Ulrich Zwingli, whose reformation in Zurich provided an alternative to Luther's, worked within the framework of the *ordo missae*. Zwingli published *An Attack on the Canon of the Mass (De canone missae epichiresis,* 1523) a few months before Luther's *Formula Missae.* Like Luther's *Formula Missae,* this was a conservative work that retained much of the Latin mass in Latin; but Zwingli replaced the Canon with four Latin prayers: a thanksgiving, an invocation of the Holy Spirit to grant the benefits of holy communion, a memorial of the passion of Christ, and a prayer for worthy reception. More strongly influenced by Renaissance humanism than Luther, Zwingli objected to the illogical and repetitious character of the Canon of the mass and appealed to patristic models in drafting his prayers. Zwingli also instituted daily preaching services based on the medieval pulpit office of Prone.

In 1525 Zwingli provided a German service for the Lord's Supper in his *Action or Use of the Lord's Supper (Action oder Brauch des Herren Nachtmal),* which prescribed practices more radical than anything Luther contemplated.[21] Holy communion would be celebrated four times a year, ministers would preside in clerical street garb rather than in liturgical vestments, and the altar would be replaced with a communion table from which the bread and wine would be administered to the people in their seats using wooden trays and cups. But the order of service still loosely followed the form of the mass. There was an opening prayer, epistle and gospel lessons (although there were set readings for the quarterly Communion Service from 1 Corinthians 11 and John 6), with the Gloria in excelsis after the epistle and the Apostles' Creed after the gospel, an exhortation to the communicants, the Lord's Prayer, a prayer for the worthy manifestation of the body of Christ as the church, the institution narrative, the ministration of communion by deacons or servers, Psalm 112 after the meal, a brief post-communion thanksgiving, and a dismissal. Zwingli would have preferred the Gloria, Creed, and Psalm to be read antiphonally, but this was not countenanced by the city council, so these texts were left for the ministers to recite. There was also no music or singing in worship in Zurich, which meant that the congregation had a very passive role in worship.

After 1525, it became evident that very different views of the Lord's Supper were held by the Swiss Reformers and the Lutherans. Their debate

---

21. See *Liturgies of the Western Church,* selected and introduced by Bard Thompson (Cleveland: World, 1961), pp. 149ff.

came to an irreconcilable climax at the Marburg Colloquy of 1529.[22] This is not the place in which to explore the disagreements between the Wittenberg and Swiss Reformers on the real presence of Christ in the sacrament. But it should be noted that the disagreement had liturgical consequences in terms of the manner of administration of the sacrament. Lutherans continued to kneel in adoration of the Christ present in the sacrament and in humble gratitude for the gift of forgiveness, life, and salvation received in the sacrament. The mass was not viewed as a dramatic reenactment of Calvary, as it had been in medieval interpretation; neither was it a dramatic reenactment of the Last Supper, as it became in Reformed practice. So great was the concern in Reformed practice to replicate what was done in the upper room that in some Reformed celebrations, notably in Scotland, communicants sat around tables to share the bread and wine. The Reformed tradition also emphasized the fellowship aspect of the Lord's Supper (the Christians' meal) and strove to include the whole congregation in the celebration (which is the reason for quarterly communions), whereas the Lutherans continued to emphasize reception as a matter of individual conscience and to celebrate the Lord's Supper whenever there were communicants.

A more mediating theological position and liturgical practice were taken up by Martin Bucer of Strassburg. Bucer had implemented there a German service of Word and Sacrament celebrated every Sunday (at least in the cathedral) with congregational singing of metrical psalms and canticles.[23] This service began with a congregational confession of sins, followed by words of pardon; then a psalm, hymn, Kyrie, or Gloria was sung, and a collect for illumination was offered. A chapter of a Gospel was read, followed by a sermon. Alms were then collected, and the communion elements were prepared on the table while the Apostles' Creed was sung. The communion office included intercessions, a consecration prayer, the Lord's Prayer, an exhortation, the words of institution, and the fraction. During the administration of the elements, psalms or hymns were sung. After a post-communion collect, the Nunc dimittis was sometimes sung, followed by the Aaronic benediction and dismissal.

This form became the basis of the French service prepared by John Calvin for the French congregation in Strasbourg (1540) and for *La forme*

---

22. See Hermann Sasse, *This Is My Body: Luther's Contention for the Real Presence in the Sacrament of the Altar* (Minneapolis: Augsburg, 1959), pp. 134ff.

23. *Liturgies of the Western Church*, pp. 167ff.

de prieres et chantz ecclesiastique avec la maniere d'administer les sacrements (1542).[24] Impressed by the singing of metrical psalms in the German congregation in Strassburg, Calvin had Clement Marot provide metrical psalms for his French-speaking congregation in Strasbourg. When Calvin returned to Geneva, Marot continued working on the French psalter. Marot died in 1544, and Theodore Beza completed the full Geneva Psalter in 1551. Calvin also secured the services of the composer Louis Bourgeois to provide tunes for these psalms. The complete French Psalter, *Pseaumes de David* (Paris, 1562), contained 125 tunes, 70 of them composed by Bourgeois. Calvin's liturgy was more celebrative than Zwingli's, but he was never able to institute a weekly celebration of the Lord's Supper in Geneva. The city council preferred to remain in uniformity with other Swiss Reformed cities by celebrating the Lord's Supper four times a year. This affected the liturgical order. Calvin demonstrated that the full service required Word and Sacrament by using the ante-communion for the typical Sunday service. Hence, the intercessions and Lord's Prayer (in paraphrase) concluded the liturgy of the Word in Calvin's service. Also, Calvin moved the institution narrative to a place before the consecration prayer so that it would serve as a warrant for the celebration and not suggest an act of consecration.

This order was further adapted by John Knox, who was resident in Geneva during the reign of Queen Mary Tudor of England. He translated it into English, and it became the rite of the Church of Scotland when The Book of Common Order supplanted The Book of Common Prayer in 1562.[25] Knox supplied new intercessions and a new prayer of consecration. The influence of the 1552 Book of Common Prayer is still detectable in the exhortation to communicants. Calvin's influence is evident in the fact that the ante-communion remained the chief Sunday service when holy communion was not celebrated. The first communion rubric in The Book of Common Order directed that holy communion be celebrated once a month, but in practice it was celebrated four times a year as in Geneva and Zurich. The church year was abolished, so communion Sundays were fixed on the first Sundays of March, June, September, and December. Among the Scots Presbyterians preparation for holy communion sometimes took several days; this became the basis of camp meetings on the American frontier.

24. *Liturgies of the Western Church*, pp. 197ff.
25. *Liturgies of the Western Church*, pp. 295ff.

Anglican Liturgy

England's leading liturgical reformer, Thomas Cranmer, archbishop of Canterbury (1533-1555), had ties with the continental Reformation extending back to his visit to Nürnberg as King Henry VIII's envoy to the court of Emperor Charles V. He married (privily) the niece of that city's celebrated Lutheran pastor, Andreas Osiander. Because the king remained theologically and liturgically conservative in spite of his break with the papacy over the matter of his divorce from Queen Catherine, Cranmer was not able to introduce real reforms until the end of Henry's reign. The gradual introduction of liturgical changes during the 1540s presents a fascinating case study in liturgical change, which space precludes chronicling here. But a significant aspect of this process was making available English translations of a number of documents from the continental Reformation, the most important of which was the Cologne church order, prepared by Bucer and Melanchthon for Archbishop Hermann von Wied, which was translated into English as *A Simple and Religious Consultation* (1547, revised 1548). Also in 1548, Cranmer himself translated into English the Lutheran catechism of Justus Jonas.[26]

After the death of Henry VIII in 1547, reform proceeded more quickly. In January 1548, candles at Candlemas, ashes on Ash Wednesday, and palms on Palm Sunday were all suppressed. In March 1548, an *Order of Communion* in English, based on material in the *Consultation* of Archbishop Hermann, was interpolated within the Latin mass at the moment of communion. It consisted of the use of one of two exhortations, confession and absolution, the "comfortable words," a "prayer of humble access," the words of administration of the sacrament, and a communion blessing. Communion was administered under both kinds.

This period of experimentation came to an end with the publication of *The Booke of Common Prayer and Administration of the Sacraments, and other Rites and Ceremonies of the Churche, after the Use of the Churche of England* (1549).[27] This remarkable achievement, for which Cranmer was

---

26. See Henry Eyster Jacobs, *The Lutheran Movement in England during the Reigns of Henry VIII and Edward VI, and Its Literary Monuments*, rev. ed. (Philadelphia: General Council Publication House, 1908).

27. See *The First and Second Prayer Books of King Edward VI*, Everyman's Library 448 (London: Dent; New York: Dutton, 1910).

largely responsible, contained in one volume all the liturgical orders that would be used in a parish church, all in English, including "The Supper of the Lorde and The Holy Communion, commonly called the Masse." While there had previously been five liturgical uses in England, an Act of Uniformity passed by Parliament decreed that the whole realm would have but one. It was the most extensive territorial imposition of liturgical uniformity in the Western Church up to that point and helped to make the speech of London ("the king's English") normative for the whole realm.

This first prayer book of King Edward VI was not just a translation and revision of the medieval Use of Sarum; it drew upon several important German church orders. In the order of mass the prayer book uses whole psalms as introits, as in Luther's *Deutsche Messe*. In translating the collects Cranmer sometimes worked from the texts in the German church orders as well as from the Latin originals. Phrases in the prayer "for the whole state of Christes church," which took the place of the *Te igitur* in the Canon, are derived from Archbishop Hermann's *Consultation*, as are the formulas taken over from the previously published communion rite. The institution narrative is similar to the one in the Brandenburg-Nüremberg church order (1533). As in the communion instructions in Luther's *Formula Missae*, the communicants are directed to go into the chancel during the offertory. The unique feature of this English mass, of course, is Cranmer's masterly reworking of the Roman Canon to express evangelical content.[28]

It seemed, however, that no one was satisfied with the prayer book. It crystallized popular resentment that had been building against religious changes since the "Pilgrimage of Grace" in 1536. The clergy of Oxfordshire refused to use it, and riots and rebellions broke out in many counties. But some thought it had not gone far enough, and the Reformation proceeded apace. In order to prevent priests from offering the sacrifice of the mass using the new communion service, the Council of Regents ordered on November 23, 1550 that all altars throughout the realm be destroyed and replaced with tables. Conservative bishops who would not countenance such measures, such as Stephen Gardiner of Winchester and Edmund Bonner of London, were imprisoned and replaced by more radical bishops, such as John Hooper and Nicholas Ridley. Cranmer also invited to England

---

28. See Aidan Kavanagh, *The Concept of Eucharistic Memorial in the Canon Revisions of Thomas Cranmer, Archbishop of Canterbury 1533-1556* (St. Meinrad, Ind.: Abbey Press, 1964).

leading Reformers from abroad. Martin Bucer was given a professorship at Cambridge, and Peter Martyr taught at Oxford. Melanchthon was also offered an Oxford professorship, but he was unable to accept it because of the crisis of the Interim in Germany. Bucer especially, in his *Censura supra libro sacrorum seu ordinationis Ecclesiae atque ministerii in regno Angliae* (1550), provided a thorough examination of the English prayer book with suggestions for revisions.[29]

A second prayer book was published in 1552, which reflected the influences of the radical bishops and the Reformers from abroad. The number of holy days in the calendar was reduced. The communion table was placed in the middle of the chancel so that communicants could be gathered around it, with the celebrant presiding "on the north side" facing some of the people. The Kyrie became a response to the rehearsal of the Ten Commandments, and the Gloria in excelsis was relocated to the post-communion section. The prayer "for the whole state of Christ's church" was removed from the eucharistic prayer and placed at the offertory. The invitation, confession of sins, absolution, and "comfortable words" were relocated from before the administration of holy communion to before the *Sursum corda*. The prayer of humble access was relocated from before the communion to after the Sanctus so that the words of institution could lead directly to the distribution of the sacrament, as in Luther's *Deutsche Messe*. The "Lamb of God" was suppressed entirely out of concern to avoid adoration of the elements. While the posture for receiving communion remained kneeling, a rubric was inserted at John Knox's insistence, but over Cranmer's objections, that denied any sense of veneration of the elements (the so-called "Black Rubric" because it was a last-minute addition printed in black ink — rubrics are usually printed in red). Communion of the sick from the reserved sacrament was abolished.

The 1552 prayer book was short-lived because the young King Edward died in 1553 and was succeeded by the Catholic Mary Tudor, who restored the Roman rite and deposed the leading reform bishops. Cranmer, Hooper, Latimer, and Ridley were imprisoned, tried for heresy, and burned at the stake in Oxford. But with the accession of Elizabeth I in 1558, the Book of Common Prayer was restored and once again imposed for use throughout the whole realm by the Act of Uniformity of 1559. The 1559 prayer book was essentially

29. See E. C. Whitaker, *Martin Bucer and the Book of Common Prayer*, Alcuin Club Collections No. 55 (Great Wakering: Mayhew-McCrimmon, 1974).

the 1552 prayer book, with the "Black Rubric" deleted. (It was restored, with revisions, in 1662.) The formulas of administration from the two previous prayer books were joined together to make possible an expression of the sacramental union of the body and blood of Christ with the bread and wine, as well as the Calvinist idea of "spiritual eating and drinking." The Elizabethan prayer book thus reflected the policy of "comprehension" of Elizabeth's reign, designed to bring all Protestants (with the exception of the Anabaptists) into one national church with a liturgy that was at once Catholic and Reformed.[30]

The Legacy of the Reformation

Much historical experience stands between us at the end of the twentieth century and the sixteenth-century Reformation. We are influenced as much, if not more, by evangelical pietism, Enlightenment rationalism, and frontier revivalism as by the Reformation.[31] The modern liturgical movement, which sought to get behind the Middle Ages to the patristic sources of the liturgy, also had to get behind the Reformation — precisely because of the degree of its historical continuity with the Middle Ages. Nevertheless, there are certain commonalities between the ideals of the modern liturgical movement and the Reformation: for example, the concern to express in worship an explicit rather than an implicit faith; the struggle to achieve a truly communal spirit in the liturgy; the emphasis on the priesthood of the faithful; agitation for the vernacular and inculturation; and a prominent role for congregational song in the liturgy.[32] Under the influence of the liturgical movement the historic forms of worship, especially the order of the mass, were revived in the churches of the Reformation. The liturgical movement has restored to the evangelical mass the reading of the Old Testament, litanized intercessions in place of the general pastoral prayers, an enacted greeting of peace before the offertory, and full eucharistic prayers.[33]

---

30. See Frank C. Senn, "Lutheran and Anglican Liturgies: Reciprocal Influences," *Anglican Theological Review* 64 (1982): 47-60.

31. See James F. White, *Protestant Worship: Traditions in Transition* (Louisville: Westminster/John Knox Press, 1989).

32. See Ernest Benjamin Koenker, *The Liturgical Renaissance in the Roman Catholic Church,* 2nd ed. (St. Louis: Concordia, 1964).

33. See Frank C. Senn, ed., *New Eucharistic Prayers: An Ecumenical Study of Their Development and Structure* (Mahwah: Paulist Press, 1986).

This historic order can no longer be presumed to be intact in the churches of the Reformation (except in the Episcopal/Anglican Churches in which the use of the prayer book is required by canon law). The pressure is great for these churches to devise "alternative" or "creative" liturgies that will be "seeker friendly." What these well-intentioned efforts run the risk of doing, however, is undermining *orthodoxia* — the "right praise" of trinitarian worship that is expressed in the texts of the historic order of service.[34] The "glory and praise" choruses and Jesus-songs in neo-evangelical worship (usually called "celebrations") do not offer the same sturdy articulations of the trinitarian faith expressed in the texts of either the Latin chants or the chorales of the German Lutheran song mass *(Lied Messe).* No matter how conducive to engendering liturgical enthusiasm the "glory and praise" choruses might be, they are theologically unequal to the *Gloria in excelsis Deo* or *Allein Gott in der Höh sei ehr.* The experience of the Reformation teaches us that the forms of public worship are not matters of indifference (adiaphora) because prayer (especially sung prayer and praise) forms belief; or, as the church fathers would have said, the *lex orandi* establishes the *lex credendi.* It is not adequate to claim the evangelical freedom to change forms of worship if those changes diminish expressions of the ecumenical dogmas of God the Holy Trinity and the two natures of Christ on which Luther, Zwingli, Calvin, Cranmer, and the Council of Trent were not in disagreement. The catholic faith requires catholic worship.

The experience of the Reformation also teaches us that when liturgy goes awry the problem may be less with its form and content than with the way in which it is celebrated and interpreted. Today historic forms of worship are being jettisoned in favor of "alternative liturgies" that employ popular-type songs and dramas with the argument that traditional liturgy is boring or meaningless to occasional (and sometimes even to regular) worshipers. Almost invariably this argument is put forward by pastors who have little competence in presiding at the liturgy in a knowledgeable or compelling way and who may even be insecure in the role of presiding minister. This ritual incompetence includes not only poor public performances by ministers, musicians, and congregations but also poor judgment on the part of worship planners in deciding what to add to or subtract from the orders provided in the authorized worship books. Many liturgies

34. See Frank C. Senn, " 'Worship Alive': An Analysis and Critique of 'Alternative Worship Services,' " *Worship* 69 (1995): 194-224.

Frank C. Senn

get bogged down in extraneous details not specified by the order, or go in uncertain directions ritually and therefore also theologically. It is little wonder that they fail to engage contemporary worshipers. As to the argument that the liturgy is boring, the historic Western liturgy does not suffer from a monotonous sameness; it has a built-in principle of variation in the rites, customs, and textual and musical options of the church year. As far as meaning is concerned, Joseph Jungmann taught that "Mass properly celebrated is itself the best catechesis."[35] The liturgy has served for centuries as the "school of the church"[36] in which one learns the faith by gathering with the community of faith to praise the Creator, by attending to the proclamation and exposition of the word of God in Scripture, by professing one's faith in public and praying for the needs of the world, by offering the world to God in a sacrifice of praise and thanksgiving, and by receiving the gifts of creation — bread and wine — as the means of communion with Christ. Only if these ritual acts are intact can there be adequate catechesis or teaching based on them.

One of the great concerns today is liturgical inculturation — liturgy reaching into the culture of the people who celebrate it. The catholic form of worship known as the mass links contemporary Christians with the people of God in all the preceding generations and provides examples of inculturation in the past. The mass is not a static form but one that is able to absorb the cultural contributions of all the societies in which it has been celebrated. This catholic form of worship was capable of being adapted to the vernacular cultures of Western Europe in the sixteenth century without being captured by those cultures, as Luther proved in his *German Mass* and as Cranmer proved in his prayer books. Both liturgies are examples of inculturation that have transcended their own time and place. This catholic form of worship has provided a link with the arts and the natural world, especially in the employment of music, iconography, and architecture. Yet, unlike free liturgies, it has resisted being taken captive by the vitalities at work in secular culture.

35. Josef A. Jungmann, *The Mass: An Historical, Theological, and Pastoral Survey*, ed. Mary Ellen Evans, trans. Julian Fernandes, S.J. (Collegeville: Liturgical Press, 1976), p. 263.
36. See Philip H. Pfatteicher, *The School of the Church: Worship and Christian Formation* (Valley Forge: Trinity Press International, 1995).

The Problem of Authority in the Church

Carl E. Braaten

ECCLESIOLOGY IS a relatively new discipline in the history of Christian dogmatics. This does not mean that there has been a lack of reflection on the church in the ancient and medieval traditions, only that a particular locus *de ecclesia* was missing from systematic treatises of theology until quite late. For example, Peter Lombard's *Four Books of Sentences,* which served as the model textbook of medieval theology, did not contain a special section on ecclesiology, nor did the *Summa Theologiae* of Thomas Aquinas. Not until the period of the Reformation was ecclesiology built into the very structure of dogmatics. Philip Melanchthon included a section *de ecclesia* in the second edition (1535) of his *Loci Communes,* and John Calvin's *Institutes of the Christian Religion* devoted Book Four exclusively to the doctrine of the church. Matching responses were elicited from Catholic theologians of the Counter-Reformation. For centuries most of the writings on the church from Catholic and Protestant theologians tended to be polemical and focused on controversial issues.

Something new has happened in the twentieth century. In 1927 Lutheran Bishop Otto Dibelius wrote a book entitled *Das Jahrhundert der Kirche* ("The Century of the Church"), which set the stage for new thinking about the church, drawing from biblical, patristic, and liturgical scholarship as well as from modern ecumenical and missionary experience. The greatest leap forward was made by the Second Vatican Council (1962-1965), which placed ecclesiology at the center. The old controversial style was replaced by an ecumenical orientation, stressing what Catholics, Orthodox, and

Protestants believe in common concerning the mystery of the church. Since then we have witnessed a vast outpouring of writings coming from all traditions dealing with the church.[1] Romano Guardini, the German Catholic theologian, said it well: "An event of incalulable importance has begun: the church is awakening in people's souls."[2]

In this century we are learning the lesson taught so eloquently by the ancient fathers, for example, by Tertullian, Cyprian, Origen, and Augustine: "We cannot have God for our father unless we have the church for our mother."[3] The notion of the church as mother was taken over by the Reformers, Luther and Calvin. In his *Large Catechism* Luther said that the Holy Spirit "has a unique community in the world. It is the mother that begets and bears every Christian through the Word of God."[4] And John Calvin said in his *Institutes of the Christian Religion:* "As our present design is to treat of the *visible* church, we may learn from the title *mother,* how useful and even necessary it is for us to know her; since there is no other way of entrance into life, unless we are conceived by her, born of her, nourished at her breast, and continually preserved under her care and government till we are divested of this mortal flesh and 'become like the angels.'"[5]

The image of the church as our mother underlines the mediating role of the church in God's work of salvation. Many theologians gulp hard at Cyprian's proposition: "Outside the church there is no salvation" *(extra ecclesiam nulla salus).* Rightly understood we would surely want to say the same thing. Reformation Christians eagerly confess salvation in Christ alone *(solus Christus).* But Christ and his church cannot be separated, for the church is the body of which Christ is the head. Catholics do not believe in a headless body, and Protestants do not believe in a bodyless head. Christ and his church are one, as the head and body are one.

1. See the very helpful bibliography compiled by Avery Dulles and Patrick Granfield, *The Church* (Wilmington, Del.: Michael Glazier, 1985).

2. Cited by Joseph Ratzinger, "The Ecclesiology of the Second Vatican Council," *Church, Ecumenism and Politics* (New York: Crossroad, 1988), p. 3.

3. Henri de Lubac provides numerous citations from the fathers in *The Motherhood of the Church* (San Francisco: Ignatius Press, 1982).

4. Martin Luther, *Large Catechism, Book of Concord* (Philadelphia: Fortress Press, 1959), p. 416.

5. John Calvin, *Institutes of the Christian Religion,* trans. John Allen (Philadelphia: Philadelphia Board of Christian Education, 1813), book 4, chap. 1, pp. 273-74.

Evangelical Protestantism is centered in the gospel. That is what the word "evangelical" means, to be defined by the evangel, the good news of the gospel. But where does the church fit in? Many evangelicals, feeling the insufficiency of a "gospel reductionism," are attempting to retrieve more churchly elements from the great tradition. Some in their search have ended up taking the path that leads back to Rome, Canterbury, or Constantinople. They realize that there is no gospel apart from the church and its sacramental life. The church is the creature of the Word; the Word is prior. But in the order of human experience the church comes before the gospel. We might put it this way: in the order of being *(ordo essendi)* the gospel comes before the church, but in the order of knowledge *(ordo cognoscendi)* the church comes before the gospel. In any case, they belong together. There is no such thing as churchless Christianity, for that would posit the possibility of relating personally to Christ without being a member of his body, the church. In the New Testament and in the theology of the fathers, to be a Christian and to be a member of the body of Christ are one and the same thing.

Images of the Church

We are in the midst of a lot of flux and ferment of thought on the church. From the traditions of biblical and patristic theology we have received many different images of the church, from which mutually contradictory implications may be derived. *Lumen Gentium* of Vatican II opened the floodgates to new ecclesiologies. Some are felt to be threatening to the ecclesiastical hierarchy and the teaching authority of the pope and bishops. — for example, the liberation theology of Leonardo Boff, the ecumenical postmodern relativism of Hans Küng, the feminist egalitarianism of Elisabeth Schüssler Fiorenza, as well as the *communio* ecclesiology of J.-M. R. Tillard.

Theologians who aim to do theology today within the broad framework of the catholic and orthodox traditions of the church — and evangelical theologians should count themselves among these if they strive to be faithful to the fundamental intention of the Reformation — are equipped with no ecclesiological *dogma* from the ancient church. We have received definitive dogmas on the Trinity and Christology but none on the church. The Russian Orthodox theologian, Georges Florovsky, admitted as much. In an important essay entitled *Le corps du Christ vivant,* he began his reflections with these words: "It is almost impossible to begin with a precise definition of the church because, to tell the truth, there is none that can pretend to enjoy recognized doctrinal authority. We can find no such definition in Holy Scripture, the Fathers, or the decrees and canons of the Ecumenical Councils."[6] And yet the reality of the church as experienced and lived out is the indispensable foundation of the entire dogmatic edifice constructed by the ancient teachers of the faith. Instead of a precise dogmatic definition they passed on a total vision of the church. Florovsky writes: "One need not define what is absolutely self-evident. The church is more a reality which one lives than an object that one analyzes and studies. Father Serge Boulgakoff put it so well, 'Come and see; one can conceive of the church only through experience, by grace in sharing in its life.'"[7]

Theologians will inevitably write about the church based on their own existential experience and reflect the particular church tradition that mothers them. Yet one can also at the same time learn from other traditions. As a Lutheran Christian I experienced and learned to think of the church as "creature of the Word" *(creatura verbi)* and as a fellowship of forgiven sinners *(communio sanctorum),* but ongoing ecumenical experience has taught me to appreciate the images and experiences of the church in Roman Catholic and Eastern Orthodox traditions. They are not monolithic; each offers a fantastic plurality of ideas and symbols of the church. From Roman Catholics we have received perspectives on the church as the mystical body of Christ and as the sacrament of salvation. From the Orthodox our ecumenical language has been enriched by understanding the church as the eucharistic community and as the icon of the Trinity. Modern biblical theology has reappropriated the concept of the church as the covenant community and as the "people of God" *(laos tou theou).* Contemporary systematic theology has promoted missiological and eschatological perspectives that stem from the rediscovery of the missionary character of the apostolic community and its link to a lively hope for the return of Christ and the ultimate triumph of God's rule and kingdom.

6. Georges Florovsky, "Le corps du Christ vivant. Une interpretation orthodoxe de l'eglisé," *La Sainte Église Universelle* (Paris: Delachaux et Niestle S.A., 1948), p. 9.
7. Florovsky, "Le corps du Christ vivant," p. 10.

Marks of the Church

In the words of the Nicene-Constantinopolitan Creed we confess: "We believe in one holy catholic and apostolic church." These are the four classical attributes of the church acknowledged by all orthodox believers in the catholic tradition. The Protestant Reformation retained this confession without any reservations whatsoever. But the situation at that time called for a new confession, and that was formulated in Article VII of the Augsburg Confession: "The church is the assembly of saints in which the Gospel is taught purely and the sacraments are administered rightly." This tells us that the one holy catholic and apostolic church can be recognized by two distinguishing marks — pure proclamation of the gospel and right administration of the sacraments. No true church can exist without them. The Augsburg Confession continues in these words: "For it is sufficient for the true unity of the Christian church that the Gospel be preached in conformity with a pure understanding of it and that the sacraments be administered in accordance with the divine Word." With these words the confessors at Augsburg believed they were being loyal to the church universal. They said: "Our churches dissent from the church catholic in no article of faith."[8] They were merely protesting against current abuses in the one church of which they were members. There was no thought that they were speaking from one church to another. The authority of the Augsburg Confession participates in the authority of the catholic tradition to which it is faithful. The Confession stated: "We have introduced nothing, either in doctrine or in ceremonies, that is contrary to Holy Scripture or the universal Christian church."[9]

Thus, when the question arises, Where is this true church, this one holy catholic and apostolic church known by the pure preaching of the gospel and the right administration of the sacraments? we do not look for it in heaven. We are not confessing our belief in an invisible church but in a concrete, down-to-earth reality discernible by words and signs that can be heard and understood, seen and swallowed — quite visible stuff. The ontological attributes of the church — its unity, holiness, catholicity, and apostolicity — must be distinguished but never separated from its phenomenological marks: word and sacraments. The ontological attributes cannot be seen by the naked

8. *Augsburg Confession, Book of Concord,* ed. Theodore G. Tappert (Philadelphia: Fortress Press, 1959), p. 48.

9. *Augsburg Confession, Book of Concord,* p. 95.

57

eye. For we see many churches, not one; we see a church full of sinners, not one that is holy; we see numerous congregations, all with their particular traditions, not one that is catholic; we see contemporary communities that reflect their linguistic and cultural histories, not one that is apostolic on a New Testament model. How, then, given this plethora of communities that call themselves Christian, can we tell which are true and which are false? Are they all true? Are there no false churches, Judas-churches that betray the Lord and the gospel? False churches, that is, heretical and apostate churches, also claim to belong to the one holy catholic and apostolic church, at least some of them do. How can we tell the difference?

Our usual answer takes us in a circle. You can tell a true church by its marks of pure preaching and right administration of the sacraments, just as you can tell a leopard by its spots. But where and when does that happen? How can we tell what is "pure" and "right" from case to case? No doubt every preacher would claim to be doing things aright. I've yet to see one stand for ordination who admits believing heresy. Congregations fire preachers they think are not doing things right; but not seldom the congregations are in the wrong. Just in our own century it has happened under the Nazis, in the fight against apartheid in South Africa, and during the civil rights struggle in the United States. With stakes so high, it is clear that we are dealing with a most practical issue that bears on the very identity and integrity of the church. The church must have clear criteria, a way of making judgments and exercising discipline.

Martin Luther once made a list of seven marks of the church.[10] In addition to preaching, baptism, and holy communion, he stipulated the keys of Christian discipline and forgiveness, the offices of ministry, public worship, and the cross, that is, the sufferings of believers for their faith. The point is that for Luther word and sacraments are not the only marks. Not any kind of preaching will do; not any way of administering sacraments will suffice. There must also be the authorized offices of ministry that discern and test whether the preaching of the gospel is pure and the sacraments are administered aright. And there must also be doctrinal criteria by which discipline can be properly exercised in the church. Authoritative decision making in the church thus requires two tracks: standards of doctrine and ministers of oversight to apply them in concrete situations.

10. Martin Luther, "On the Councils and the Church," *Luther's Works*, vol. 41 (Philadelphia: Fortress Press, 1966), pp. 150-65.

The Problem of Heresy

In every age the church is called "to contend for the faith which was once for all delivered to the saints" (Jude 3). The function of the creeds and confessions is to provide standards by which the church can judge and condemn false teachings contrary to the gospel. The church has always found it necessary to draw a dividing line between what is acceptable teaching and what is unacceptable. However, heresy has become virtually outmoded in the modern church for two reasons. First, the rise of democracy meant that the church lost the coercive power of the state to punish heretics as criminals; and second, the Enlightenment brought the age of tolerance in which the rules that set limits to heresy were overthrown. Orthodoxy was put on the defensive. Heresy became a matter of religious freedom and human rights. The threat of heresy to personal salvation that prevailed in the ancient church was annulled. The issue of heresy shifted from soteriology to ecclesiology. The category of heresy could still be invoked when an extreme case threatened the unity of community. Dissent was permitted so long as it did not break the unity of the church. Not heresy but schism became the more serious concern. To prevent heresy from leading to schism, the churches today, maintaining their organizational unity at almost all costs, have taken to promoting inclusivity and diversity at the expense of revealed truth and biblical morality, pushing back the limits to heresy, to the point where people are "tossed to and fro and blown by every wind of doctrine" (Eph. 4:14).

One thing is more life-threatening to the church than heresy, and that is the unwillingness or inability to tell the difference between orthodoxy and heresy. Is this distinction truly outmoded, once heresy becomes decriminalized by the collapse of Christendom, once it is no longer subject to the state's exercise of power? I do not think so. Retrieving the category of heresy is important if the church is to be clear about its apostolic identity and confession of faith. Without it, orthodoxy becomes an endangered species.

It is often assumed that the orthodoxy/heresy distinction is an impediment to theology in an ecumenical age. Why don't we just all get together and forget our doctrinal differences? Such an attitude of presumed tolerance deals a deathblow to the ecumenical quest for the unity of the church. If there is any reality to being members of one church with one faith, of becoming one reconciled ecclesial fellowship of diverse Christian communities, there must be boundary lines. Otherwise one could not know to what one belongs — the Communist Party, the Church of Scientology, or something else. It becomes all the more necessary in a pluralistic age to set limits to pluralism. Pluralism as such is not the problem. The orthodox vision does not call for monolithic uniformitarianism. New Testament studies today make clear that while there was abundant pluralism in New Testament Christianity, there existed from the beginning a concern that the diversity of beliefs, doctrines, and practices did not threaten the basic unity of eucharistic fellowship of believers, grounded in the truth of the gospel. It was the task of the apostolic *paradosis* and ministry to safeguard the essential bonds of unity and continuity as the church passed from one generation to another.

Heretical teachings are not always easily distinguishable from sound doctrines. The Arian controversy in the fourth century is particularly illuminating. Pastor Arius was a biblical theologian. He defended his teaching that Christ is neither fully God nor fully man by means of exegetical learning. Trained in the School of Lucian of Antioch, he was adept at using the grammatical and historical method of exegesis. He quickly gained the support of Eusebius of Nicomedia. Athanasius used a nonbiblical word, *homoousion,* as a test word against Arius and was reviled for being unbiblical. The Arian heretics quoted Bible passages; Athanasius and the ultimately orthodox verdict at Nicaea used novel philosophical language to articulate the biblical message as a whole, the saving truth of God's revelation in Christ. It took a long struggle to draw a clear line between orthodoxy and heresy, but without it Christianity would have been dissolved into another Hellenistic mystery cult of half-divinities in human form.

The point is that heresies never advertise themselves as such. They often hide behind a mask of biblical language, sincere piety, or moral virtue and are promoted by a well-organized network of like-minded fanatics on a mission to convert the church to their point of view. Heresies never circulate with a surgeon general's warning that swallowing them might impair one's spiritual health.

Structures of Authority

The first two instruments developed by the church to exclude heresy and establish orthodoxy were the canon of Scripture and dogma. The Reformation concurred in the judgments of the ancient church concerning the authority of Scripture and dogma. These judgments provide the definitive interpretation of Scripture on certain doctrines contested by heresies that threatened the access of believers to the saving revelation of God in Jesus Christ. In post-Reformation Protestantism, the tendency arose to set the Bible against the church and its tradition. Protestant biblicism, with its inflated doctrines of literal inerrancy and verbal inspiration, first evolved as a polemic against the equally inflated infallibility of the papal office and then hardened itself into fundamentalist rigidities in the fight against modernism. The Reformation view of the relation of Scripture to the church is more catholic, not as an either/or relation but as a structural conjunction of both/and.

Today we need to stress the church-relatedness of Scripture on two fronts: against Protestant biblicist fundamentalism, on the one side, and against modern rationalist historicism, which uses the historical-critical method to deconstruct the Scriptures as the "book of the church," on the other. Both fundamentalism and historicism pretend that they approach the Scriptures without presuppositions. These seemingly incompatible heresies are simply two sides of the same coin; in disregarding the church as the *Sitz im Leben* of scriptural interpretation, they proceed to look through the glasses of their own self-concealed subjectivity. In pretending to be neutral and objective, both are engaging in gross self-deception, and they deceive millions of others to boot.

Scripture exists on account of the church and for the sake of the church. Its authority derives from the same gospel that gives birth to the church, creating a symbiotic relation between Scripture and the church. The experiences and needs of the church form the appropriate heuristic principles, the *Fragestellung,* for scriptural exegesis. When scriptural interpretation takes place without regard for the church, some other worldview takes charge of the entire hermeneutical operation and invariably leads away from the gospel center of Scripture. With remarks such as these we are swimming against the current of scholarly academic consensus. Today the task of scriptural interpretation has been wrested from the church and placed in the hands of the academy or society of biblical scholars who often proceed as though the church did not exist, as though the experience and tradition of scriptural exegesis in church history count for naught.

The Scripture principle of Reformation theology and its hermeneutical principles make sense only in and with the church. Slogans such as *sola Scriptura,* analogy of faith, Scripture interprets itself, and the like are not freestanding philosophical axioms but guidelines for the church to get to the vital center of the whole of Scripture. The authority of Scripture functions not in separation from the church but only in conjunction with the Spirit-generated fruits in the life of the church, its apostolic confession of faith and its life-giving sacraments of baptism, absolution, and the Lord's Supper.

We have stressed the catholicity of the Reformation understanding of Scripture in its structural connectedness to the church. Controversy arises in the life of the church — and this was the point of difference between the German Reformers and their Roman confutators — when gospel-contradicting traditions emerge in the life of the church that exempt themselves from the prophetic critique of Scripture. The hierarchical ordering of norms in the church must grant the place of preeminent priority to the prophetic and apostolic witnesses to the gospel of Jesus Christ. Traditions created by the ongoing proclamation of the church from the Scriptures must never become independent and lord it over their master. Scripture is the source of the power that creates the church, and tradition remains the servant medium.

Dogmas and confessions are, alongside the Scriptures, the church's strongest weapon against heresies, sects, and cults. In times of crisis they hold the key to the being or nonbeing of the church. Why? Because they form a concrete and concentrated summary of the church's interpretation of Scripture. They are binding norms because *(quia)* and not merely insofar as *(quatenus)* they are a perfectly true distillation of Scripture's witness to God's saving revelation in Jesus Christ. Dogmas and confessional statements claim to represent, not the religious feelings of individuals, be they those of bishops, theologians, or charismatic lay folks, but the voice of the whole church, the *consensus fidelium*, diachronically and synchronically. They comprise the enduring and irreplaceable curriculum of the teaching church. Church doctrines are not like professorial statements about God and things of topical interest; rather, they are the church's response of faith under the guidance of the Holy Spirit to the truth claims of the gospel.

Certainly the Reformation stands decidedly on the side of the great ecumenical creeds and dogmas of the catholic tradition. All of the ancient creeds were woven into the fabric of the Reformation confessional writings. Luther was a professor of Bible, but he knew perfectly well that the teaching of the church does not consist of reciting Scripture passages. As Werner Elert says: "Luther's own exegetical works show how the exegete who is really concerned with understanding the gospel inevitably becomes a dogmatician."[11] Luther's *Small Catechism* and *Large Catechism* are proof that he built the ancient dogmas of the catholic church into the evangelical faith of the Reformation. And the same thing is true of the entire *Book of Concord.* This is why evangelical catholics are often ill at ease with standard forms of American evangelicalism. Paul Tillich spoke of the "leaping theory of Protestantism," the notion that we can leap over twenty centuries of church tradition into Bibleland. What results are a few evangelical slogans and protestant principles without the catholic substance.

Furthermore, the ancient ecumenical dogmas possess greater authority than the Augsburg Confession or any of the other Reformation confessions. In writing about the relation of the ancient symbols of the faith to the later ones, David Hollaz said: "Those which were approved with the unanimous consent of the whole Catholic Church, namely, the three ecumenical symbols, possess far greater authority than those which have received the sanction and approbation of only a few particular churches."[12] This means that the evangelical confessions of the Reformation cannot take precedence over the ecumenical creeds of the ancient church in measuring and judging the faith of the whole catholic church. The Reformers knew that; they presupposed the catholicity of the church they set out to reform. Those who forget what the Reformers knew and took for granted have virtually turned their movement into a bunch of sects.

Preaching in the church has fallen to a nearly all-time low. A major reason for this is that the teaching of the church's doctrines and confessions, once the core of the theological curriculum, has given way to all the special interests that vie for equal time. Church doctrine is the backbone of good preaching. Seminarians today are likely to leave seminary knowing more about the latest trends in theology — liberationism, feminism, multiculturalism, religious pluralism, environmentalism, etc. — which they pick up through bull sessions, than they know about the classic texts of Eastern and Western Christian thought. They are more likely to have read the popular books of Rosemary Radford Ruether, James Cone, and John Hick than such

11. Werner Elert, *The Structure of Lutheranism,* trans. Walter A. Hansen (St. Louis: Concordia, 1962), p. 201.

12. Heinrich Schmid, *The Doctrinal Theology of the Evangelical Lutheran Church,* trans. Charles A. Hay and Henry E. Jacobs (Minneapolis: Augsburg, 1961), p. 100.

classics as Origen's *On First Principles,* Augustine's *De trinitate,* and Anselm's *Cur deus homo?* The failure of theological education — I say this after spending the past four decades in the enterprise — lies in its inability to make the necessary move from the saving revelation of God in Christ attested by the Scriptures to the actual preaching of salvation in and by the church. The major reason for this failure is inattention to the missing link between Scripture and preaching — the role of dogma and confession in the historic life of the church.

Dogma and confessions always affirm and condemn. The reason so much modern preaching is boring is that it feels compelled to smile on whatever is passing by. True preaching, based on Scripture, dogma, and confession, always includes anathema, judgment, condemnation — the power of negative thinking. Dogma and confessions say not only "We believe, teach, and confess" but also "We reject and condemn all contrary teachings." Karl Barth wrote: "If we have not the confidence . . . to say *damnamus,* then we might as well omit the *credimus.* . . . If the Yes does not in some way contain the No, it will not be the Yes of a confession."[13]

The Teaching Authority of the Church

Dietrich Bonhoeffer wrote: "The concept of heresy has been lost today because there isn't any teaching authority. . . . The modern ecumenical councils are anything but councils, because the word 'heresy' has been stricken from their vocabulary."[14] Churches of the Reformation have retained some structures of authority — the authority of the Word, the Holy Scriptures, the ecumenical creeds, and their respective confessional writings. But they do not possess any effective official and public locus of authority whose task is to interpret and implement the normative sources of faith and doctrine. Leaving it all up to a voters' assembly based on representative principles is a formula for disaster. Where does the buck stop when it comes to matters of interpretation and discipline? The church must have not only normative sources written down on paper but also authoritative office-

13. Karl Barth, *Church Dogmatics,* ed. G. W. Bromiley and T. F. Torrance (Edinburgh: T & T Clark, 1956), I/2, pp. 630-31.

14. Dietrich Bonhoeffer, *Gesammelte Schriften,* vol. 3 (Munich: Kaiser Verlag, 1966), p. 206.

holders ordained to teach the whole church. Protestants do not know who these officeholders are. They seem to have vanished.

A strong sense of pastoral authority has also diminished to the vanishing point. Many newly ordained pastors think of themselves as part of the universal priesthood of all believers, nothing more. Many think that ordination authorizes a pastor to be the official representative of the congregation he or she serves. That is the theory of representative democracy, which holds that in ordination laypeople transfer rights and privileges that belong to them to a clergyperson they choose to represent them, to act in their stead and on their behalf so that things may get done decently and in order.

In sharp contrast, we would want to affirm the structural polarity of pastoral office and local congregation. The church is ontologically bipolar; it is constituted both by the *preaching* and by the *hearing* of the Word. Thus ordination is a sacramental rite signifying that a pastor is called and commissioned by the Holy Spirit to represent Christ to the people, to stand over against them as one who brings the Word of God from the outside, so to speak, that is, from beyond insights generated out of their own experience. Pastors are shepherds. Sheep do not choose their shepherds and lead them around by the nose. In Protestantism our doctrine of the relation beween shepherds and sheep has become completely confused.

Even when we have in principle — though hardly in practice — preserved a relatively high doctrine of the authority of Scripture, dogma, and confession, the chain of authority breaks at its weakest link. And that is the teaching office of the church. With the loss of the episcopal office at the time of the Reformation, the locus of authority has been wandering all over the place, now in the hands of the princes, now in the hands of a synod of ordained pastors, now in the hands of an assembly attended by an arbitrary percentage of clergy and laity. But synod assemblies cannot teach and discipline the church, its ministers and members; only persons authorized by the Spirit of God through prayer and the "laying on of hands" (1 Tim. 4:14) can do that.

Bonhoeffer was right. We have lost the teaching office of the church and seem to be afraid to reconstitute it where it belongs in terms of the catholic tradition. Article XXVIII of the Augsburg Confession says:

> According to divine right, therefore, it is the office of the bishop to preach the Gospel, forgive sins, judge doctrine and condemn doctrine that is contrary to the Gospel, and exclude from the Christian community the

ungodly whose wicked conduct is manifest. All this is to be done not by human power but by God's Word alone. On this account parish ministers and churches are bound to be obedient to the bishops according to the saying of Christ in Luke 10:16, "He who hears you hears me."

Finally, the question of the authoritative sources of Christian doctrine *in* the church cannot be separated from the teaching authority *of* the church. Many democratically elected officials have issued statements that claim to speak for the church, but their words carry no authority. Often what they say is received as a joke. The lesson to be learned is that when the church lost the backbone of its teaching office, it began to act more and more like a jellyfish. This harsh judgment brings us exactly up against the ecumenical problem par excellence, the doctrine of ordination and the office of ministry. The next rounds of ecumenical dialogue will need to search for a solution to this problem, which now stands as the chief obstacle in the way of reconciling the ministries of our separated churches.

The Pastoral Office:
A Catholic and Ecumenical Perspective

James R. Crumley

THOUGH THEY define it in a variety of ways and structure it in diverse forms, churches almost without exception have an ordained ministry. For some, such ministry is defined primarily as leadership, with the understanding that any organized group needs someone out front. For the vast majority of Christians, however, ministry is far more and is described using such terms as "indispensable," "constitutive of the church," "essential," "ordained by God." Lutherans have lived with ministry somewhat ambiguously, ready to defend its essential quality in terms of confession but allowing a great deal of latitude in describing its function within the church and its structure within the organization. In ecumenical relationships, there has been a growing consensus that different interpretations of ministry are an obstacle to fellowship or communion between church bodies. In some instances, ministry has been called the one remaining obstacle to such *koinonia*. Thus theological definitions of ministry are attempted in many places today with an announced intention to discover the fundamental place of ministry within the churches, the functions ministers fulfill, and especially the way in which ministers belong within or over against the whole people of God.

Furthermore, the culture — particularly Western culture, or perhaps even more specifically, American culture — is forcing a reassessment of the place of the churches and especially of their ministry. It is assumed by many that churches are to play a role within the society in which they live. Those expectations may be quite different from the way in which the churches see themselves and attempt to plan their program. Popularly, there are also certain expectations of the ministers of churches, and it is revealing to understand how rapidly those expectations have changed within the last few decades. Consider the following realities.

(1) Ambiguity and uncertainty are growing on the part of the churches as to who ministers are and what they are to do. In our own church we have gone through various "fads," seeing ministers as "enablers," "directors," "chief evangelists," etc. Many of our pastors as well have expressed their own insecurity about their calling by rushing after every new and different role that is proposed.

(2) Officially, in our own church, we have moved from an interpretation of the ordained ministry as a specific "calling" to that of "career." In so doing, we have reinterpreted motivation for service, and the expectations of both the pastor and the congregation have changed.

(3) This movement toward career rather than calling has imposed a different set of criteria by which success is measured. Careers in the secular domain are evaluated by production, by financial progress and growth, by the way in which the market is understood and its possibilities grasped. While faithfulness may play a part in such evaluation, it is of lower value. Furthermore, the evaluative criteria are determined by the employer, and when the congregation is seen in such terms, the pastor is seen as either a success or a failure depending on the congregation's expectations.

(4) Pastors have also been led to prescribe parameters around their own service, as to where they wish to serve, what type of congregation deserves them, what financial package can be negotiated, what employment is available for their spouse, and what the community can offer them as advantages.

(5) Pastors are seldom the best-educated and best-informed persons within a congregation. They cannot offer such credentials and often are judged insecure or inferior because of their qualifications on such grounds. Both the pastor and the congregation may lack an understanding of the specific role that the pastor fills in terms of the mission of the church as a whole.

(6) There has been a growing concern as to how laypeople serve or have ministries in the church. This concern is appropriate and needs to be pursued even more zealously. However, we have talked of lay participation to such an extent that pastors are no longer sure how and where they are

needed. For some, there has been a growing conviction that anyone in the church can do what he or she chooses to do. The pastor's liturgical role, teaching capability, program responsibility, and even preaching and sacramental roles are often questioned by both pastor and congregation. This uncertainty is not alleviated by the church as it sets expectations for its ordained clergy.

The list could go on and on, but even these reminders are sufficient to pose the problem. What is the place of the ordained ministry within the church? What role should it play?

Those questions, important as they are, cannot be answered immediately, for there are prior questions, and they have to do with the church. In American Lutheranism, we have attempted to answer fundamental questions in several areas without beginning with ecclesiology. What is the church? Is it essential in God's plan of salvation? If so, why and how? What is the mission of the church in the world today?

Within most churches, and in the writings of many theologians about the church, one can detect a growing appreciation for the church as "community," the "communion of saints," "*koinonia*," established in the Holy Spirit, made up of people baptized into the name of the triune God and participating in the life of the Trinity, the universal priesthood, a global community sent to witness in and to the whole world. Wherever the faithful have seriously considered the nature of the church, this aspect has been vital, but it is being recaptured in a new way today and is of considerable emphasis. It has much to say about ministry.

Let me cite some important references with which we may be familiar but which we need to review in terms of their implications for ministry:

Now you are the body of Christ. (1 Cor. 12:27)

The Church is the assembly of all believers in which the Gospel is preached in its purity and the holy sacraments are administered according to the Gospel. (Augsburg Confession, Article VII)[1]

The Christian Church is, properly speaking, nothing else than the assembly of all believers and saints. (Augsburg Confession, Article VIII)[2]

---

1. *The Book of Concord,* ed. Theodore Tappert (Philadelphia: Fortress, 1981), p. 32.
2. *The Book of Concord,* p. 33.

In accordance with the Scriptures, therefore, we maintain that the Church in the proper sense is the assembly of saints who truly believe the Gospel of Christ and who have the Holy Spirit. (*Apology of the Augsburg Confession*, Articles VII and VIII)[3]

He [the Holy Spirit] first leads us into his holy community, placing us upon the bosom of the Church, where he preaches to us and brings us Christ. . . . In the first place, he has a unique community in the world. It is a mother that begets and bears every Christian through the Word of God. . . . For where Christ is not preached, there is no Holy Spirit to create, call, and gather the Christian Church, and outside it no one can come to the Lord Christ. . . . I believe that there is on earth a little holy flock or community of pure saints under one head, Christ. It is called together by the Holy Spirit in one faith, mind, and understanding. It possesses a variety of gifts, yet it is united in love without sect or schism. . . . Until the last day, the Holy Spirit remains with the holy community or Christian people. (*The Large Catechism*, The Apostles' Creed, Article 3)[4]

The Church exists both as an inclusive fellowship and as congregations gathered together for worship and Christian service. Congregations find their fulfillment in the universal community of the Church and the universal Church exists in and through congregations. (*The Constitution of the Evangelical Lutheran Church in America*, 3.02)

The Church is a people created by God in Christ, empowered by the Holy Spirit, called and sent to bear witness to God's creative redeeming and sanctifying activity in the world. (*The Constitution of the Evangelical Lutheran Church in America*, 4.01)[5]

It is interesting to note that ecumenical conversations, both bilateral and multilateral, in discussing ministry have begun with assertions about the church:

In the Holy Spirit and His messengers, Christ gathers His community on earth. The Church is the community in which by faith the new life,

3. *The Book of Concord*, p. 173.
4. *The Book of Concord*, pp. 415-20.
5. "The Constitution of the Evangelical Lutheran Church in America," in *Constitution, By-Laws and Continuing Resolutions* (Minneapolis: Augsburg Fortress, 1991), pp. 20, 21.

reconciliation, justification and peace are received, lived, attested, and thus communicated to humanity.[6]

In a broken world God calls the whole of humanity to become God's people. For this purpose God chose Israel and then spoke in a unique and decisive way in Jesus Christ, God's Son. Jesus made His own the nature, condition, and cause of the whole human race, giving Himself to be a sacrifice for all. Jesus' life of service, His death and resurrection, are the foundation of the new community which is built up continually by the good news of the Gospel and the gift of the sacraments.[7]

It is also important to remember that, ecumenically, the *koinonia* that exists between Christians and the Triune God and the *koinonia* of Christians with one another is expressed constitutionally when the Lutheran World Federation calls itself a "communion of churches" and when the World Council speaks of the "fellowship" that exists between member churches. While much attention needs to be given to the meaning and implications of this emphasis, it is an important and growing recognition within and among churches. Now our question is how it ought to be applied to ministry.

In pursuing this question it is necessary to confront a prevailing idea in our culture that the church is unnecessary and that one needs simply to find a personal relationship with Jesus Christ as Lord and Savior. Consistently, polls that are taken to demonstrate the beliefs and practices of Americans show that more than 90 percent profess a belief in God, but that only about 50 percent belong to a church, and that of those who belong to churches only about one-third attend on any given Sunday. In addition, some who do profess belief in the church think of it as an unrealistic, almost ethereal entity that is not seen nor known on this earth. Their skepticism goes beyond the theological view of the hidden church or the invisible church. This view denigrates the institutional church as we know it and expresses as irrelevant or unnecessary the gathered congregation among whom the Word is preached and the sacraments administered.

In contrast, the confessional and ecumenical view of the church that I am attempting to state insists that the church, the organized church, the

6. Roman Catholic–Lutheran International Commission, *The Ministry in the Church* (Geneva: Lutheran World Federation, 1982), p. 6.

7. Faith and Order Commission, *Baptism, Eucharist and Ministry,* Paper no. 111 (Geneva: World Council of Churches, 1982), p. 20.

church as we know and see it, is integral to God's plan of salvation. That is not to say that the church never needs to be reformed and renewed, but it is to insist that the church is founded by God in Christ and that it is kept by the Holy Spirit so that even the gates of hell will not prevail against it. An incarnational theology on which we depend insists that the divine reality is embodied in the structures and forms of creation; those structures and forms bear the imperfections and problems of a fallen world but have not lost their integrity and their character as bearers of the divine revelation.

Ministry is understood, then, in the context of the church that God has founded in Christ and sustains through the Spirit. That means that the whole people of God are in ministry. They are sent into the world for the gospel, and they are sustained and empowered for their task through the gospel. Important as this principle is, however, we are still struggling to articulate it in the life of the church. Are all of the people of God called to serve the gospel, or are they called through the gospel to serve the world? Is the ministry of the whole people of God defined by the time they spend in church and the responsibilities that they fill within the church, or is that ministry rather defined by the way they live in the world, work at their occupations, and fulfill responsibilities in home and community?

The emphasis with which we begin at this point will make quite a difference in the way in which we delineate specific ministries within the church. One prevailing problem is the broad assumption that one can do within the church whatever one chooses to do. If one chooses to teach, then one must be allowed to do so. If one chooses to be a liturgical leader, then one must be given that privilege. Yet the New Testament, especially in passages such as 1 Corinthians 12, points out that God sustains his church through gifts that are given to individual members but that are given for the health and stability of the whole body. The specific tasks for which members are chosen should not be considered of higher or lower rank, for they are all necessary though they are not all the same. God chooses individuals for specific tasks or ministries through the gifts that he has given.

That brings us at once to the ordained ministry, which is termed in our title the "pastoral office." It is an office within and among the whole people of God, an office to which the Chief Shepherd calls and appoints under-shepherds. It is an office to which persons are called by their gifts and by the church's recognition that those gifts are possessed. It is an essential office without which the church does not exist, because it is an office that serves the gospel, and the gospel itself constitutes the church and calls the faithful to service. Again, let us look at our confessional and constitutional provisions:

> In order that we may obtain this faith, the ministry of teaching the Gospel and administering the sacraments was instituted.[8]

> The New Testament shows how there emerged from among the ministries a special ministry which was understood as standing in the succession of the apostles sent by Christ. Such a special ministry proved to be necessary for the sake of leadership in the communities. One can, therefore, say that according to the New Testament the "special ministry" established by Jesus Christ through the calling and sending of the apostles "was essential then — it is essential in all times and circumstances."[9]

> Our churches are thus able today to declare in common that the essential and specific function of the ordained minister is to assemble and build up the Christian community by proclaiming the word of God, celebrating the sacraments and presiding over the liturgical, missionary, and diaconal life of the community.[10]

> In order to fulfill its mission, the Church needs persons who are publicly and continually responsible for pointing to its fundamental dependence on Jesus Christ, and thereby provide, within a multiplicity of gifts, a focus of its unity. The ministry of such persons, who since very early times have been ordained, is constitutive for the life and witness of the Church.[11]

> Within the people of God and for the sake of the Gospel ministry entrusted to all believers, God has instituted the office of the ministry of Word and Sacrament.[12]

To insist on the ordained ministry as essential in the church has led in some instances to misunderstanding. On the one hand, the officeholder has sometimes been held to be superior to or above other persons in the

---

8. Augsburg Confession, Article V, in *The Book of Concord,* p. 31.

9. *The Ministry in the Church,* par. 17, p. 8.

10. *The Ministry in the Church,* par. 31, p. 14.

11. *Baptism, Eucharist and Ministry,* p. 21.

12. "The Constitution of the Evangelical Lutheran Church in America," 7.21, p. 28.

church. This view has led some pastors to become tyrants and to insist that all things in the parish must be done exactly in accordance with their wishes. At times this attitude has resulted in a subservient role for the layperson and in the view that the ordained ministry exists apart from the whole people of God. But, on the other hand, to view the office as essential has not precluded an inferior view of it and of the people who hold it. After all, some of the essential roles in society are considered inferior, and you simply have to find the people to do the chores. Thus, the pastor may be thought of as the "hired help" of the parish. Both wrong understandings fail to take into account that the church is a community, a community of differentiated relationships of mutual service.

The office is differentiated, in that it has specific responsibilities and functions. However, even while we recognize this fact and emphasize the office's function, I do not want completely to dismiss ontological nuances to the one who fills the office. We do not make ordination a sacrament, though Melanchthon was of the opinion that it might appropriately be so designated. There is certainly a sacramental quality to it, regardless of how else we may view it. There is the promised grace of God, the gift given through the laying on of hands, and the understanding that God makes possible our doing what he calls us to do. While ordination does not bestow an indelible character, it nonetheless sets a particular person apart to do a specific work with the community, and the person is authorized to take certain responsibilities. The community itself agrees to this designation, to the location of this person within the community. Furthermore, the ordinand takes a vow to lead the people of God "by your own example in faithful service and holy living."

Note that I have said that there are "specific" responsibilities that the person who fills the pastoral office assumes. If this office has been denigrated within our culture, even within our church, we must admit that we pastors have to bear some of the blame. We have not always understood the specific and essential nature of our office. We have tried to become all things to all people, and not in the good sense in which Paul used the term. In sensing the need for administration, we have tried to become managers. We have tried to become amateur psychologists in order to assist people with their problems. We have tried to become programmatic experts to fill the expectations of our diverse congregation as to what individuals assume that they need. And we have allowed the culture to define what the church's culture ought to be. We have not always understood that preaching the

Word of God requires the very best of which we are capable, and we have not always struggled with those hard issues of the modern context so as to help our people understand the challenges that confront them. We have not had the confidence of our office to understand the central place of preaching and administering the sacraments in the life of the community so that our people have not been nurtured in the way open to them.

In some sense, I suppose we could say that the trouble is that we have not been "professional" enough and have not understood the implications of "career" enough. I hesitate to speak of the ministry in such terms, but even those who use these terms which are not completely appropriate to the ordained ministry call for the attention that others of us insist upon. The professional person is one who understands what one's profession is, what it entails, how one does it effectively. To say that I am a pastor in the church means that I am accountable first of all to Jesus Christ himself, but that accountability also includes the specific tasks for which I am responsible, that I have vowed to do, and that I am expected to perform and to perform effectively.

While the ministry of deacon is an important one in the church, I am passing over it lightly simply because my primary emphasis is the pastoral ministry. I think that the establishment of the diaconate is appropriate for the Evangelical Lutheran Church in America (ELCA) at the present time. I also think that the refusal to ordain deacons is appropriate now, because there is no concise description as to which servants of the church should be included in the category of deacons. When in our ELCA experience we can be clear as to the functions of the persons in that office with a specific understanding of who can be included and for what reasons, I believe that ordination might be most appropriate.

I consider the office of bishop to be an important part of the pastoral office that needs more attention among us. We have bishops, it is true, and the office has evolved in a good way in the little more than a decade that we have been using the title. But more specificity is needed. In particular, we need to articulate more fully that servants in the church must have the authority to do what the office demands. We need to think carefully about the authority needed by those who do oversight.

> The Church as the body of Christ and the eschatological people of God is constituted by the Holy Spirit through a diversity of gifts or ministries. Among these gifts a ministry of episcope is necessary to express and

75

safeguard the unity of the body. Every church needs this ministry of unity in some form in order to be the Church of God, the one body of Christ, a sign of the unity of all in the kingdom.[13]

We need to remember that the Lutheran Reformers of the sixteenth century did not assume that *episcope* could be done away with or that bishops were not needed. They assumed that, since bishops as the church defined them were not available in their situation, some other provision had to be made. But their intention and desire was to keep the episcopacy. Their solution was seen as a temporary and emergency measure.

Currently, in the proposals from the Lutheran-Episcopal dialogue, we Lutherans are asked to adopt a form of the episcopacy deemed essential by some other churches. That form has to do with the historic succession. We claim to have, and rightly so, the apostolic succession in the gospel. The Episcopal Church acknowledges our succession in the gospel, and thus acknowledges our ministry. According to our confessions and our history, we cannot consider the historic succession in the episcopacy essential; however, we know that persons who have been ordained into it have had a valid ministry. Many of our Lutheran churches have maintained or have adopted the historic succession. As an expression of the *koinonia* that exists among Lutheran churches and to open doors in ecumenical relationships, I believe that the ELCA ought to adopt and implement those proposals which would over time include our ordained ministry in the line of historic succession.

But there is a reason for accepting these proposals even beyond the value of ecclesial relationships, it seems to me. We live in a time when the culture of the church confronts the culture of the society in an almost dramatic way. Ours is an alien culture; we use language, ceremonies, and rites that are foreign to the world in which we exist. But we cannot compromise the culture of our church, of our faith. In fact, symbols and expressions that in some times might be of lesser importance are now in these times of greater importance. I believe that our acknowledgment not only of the tradition of the spoken word but also of the tradition of episcopacy that has been given the responsibility of proclaiming that word and guarding its purity could be of value to our witness. Our task as a church is to maintain a tradition, for the revelation of God has been given in a moment of history.

13. *Baptism, Eucharist and Ministry,* p. 25.

In celebrating our heritage as children of the Reformation, we are giving appropriate attention to ministry within the church of Jesus Christ, and particularly to the pastoral office. In so doing, we discover anew that we are part of a catholic tradition that takes into account the mission of the church as described or mandated in the Bible and as developed over the centuries. Such an examination must lift high the essential quality of word and sacrament in the intention of God and in the lives of people. Thus the people of the church can appropriately understand the task of pastors as servants of the gospel, as ministers of and to the whole people of God, and as under-shepherds of that great Shepherd of the sheep.

Lutheran Pietism and Catholic Piety

Robert L. Wilken

FOR SOME years it has been my custom to listen to Johann Sebastian Bach's St. Matthew Passion on Good Friday. I suppose this goes back to a time when Good Friday was a day of high solemnity. Even the hours of the day were holy. It was not enough simply to go to church; the day itself was to be marked with reverence. During my childhood it was the one day of the year that we went to church in the morning and then again in the evening, and in the afternoon we were expected to spend our time quietly meditating on Jesus' final hours on the cross. In those days I did not listen to Bach (though of course we sang Bach chorales in church), but as I have learned to love Bach's music, it has seemed that the discipline of listening to the entire Passion on Good Friday was one way of keeping faith with older ways.

In recent years I have begun to observe a similar custom during the Christmas season, and that is to listen to the Christmas Oratorio in its entirety. After the rush of the days before Christmas, crowded with shopping and wrapping presents, cooking and decorating the house, there comes a time of peace and serenity on the day after Christmas. In the days that follow, the twelve days of Christmas that culminate in the Feast of the Epiphany, Bach's Christmas Oratorio allows me to meditate on the great mystery we celebrate in that holy season: that the Blessed Virgin gives birth to the boundless and ineffable God, and the earth offers a cave to the unapproachable One.

There are many similarities between the two works — the use of some of the same chorale melodies (it is always a surprise to hear "O Sacred

Head" during Christmas), the crisp recitatives drawn from the Gospels to give a narrative setting for the arias, stately and meditative choruses, and of course the *cantus firmus* of Bach's faith and devotion reflected in the arias. Yet the more I have listened to the two works, the more I have felt the differences, not in the obvious way that Holy Week and Christmas call for different music — there is much more brass in the Christmas Oratorio, for example — but in the way Bach gives voice to his piety.

No doubt these differences, if they are in fact differences, are due in part to the subject matter of the two works, the passion and death of Christ and the birth of Christ. In the St. Matthew Passion, Bach seems to be working with familiar Lutheran themes: Christ's vicarious suffering, his death as a sacrificial offering for the sins of humankind, sorrow and remorse over our sins, the Christ "for us," as in the early aria "Buss und Reu knirscht das Sündenherz entzwei" (Repentance and sorrow rend the sinful heart in two), and related themes. The work is, of course, punctuated with passion chorales, for example, "Herzliebster Jesus, was hast du verbrochen, Dass man ein solch hart Urteil hat gesprochen" (Dearest Jesus, what law have you broken that you are judged so harshly), that express similar ideas.

To be sure, in the St. Matthew Passion there are some arias in which the "Christ for us" gives way to the "Christ in us" and Bach displays a certain Jesus-mysticism. Immediately after the narration of the Last Supper he inserts a soprano aria that begins "Ich will dir mein Herze schenken" (I want to give you my heart) and continues "Senke dich, mein Heil, hinein" (Settle deep within me, O Savior). And after Peter says that he will not deny Christ, Bach placed the chorale "Ich will hier bei dir stehen," which ends with the words "Alsdann will ich dich fassen in meinen Arm und Schoss" (I will grasp you in my arms and bosom). And, of course, there is the final bass aria after Christ has died: "Mache dich, meine Herze, rein, Ich will Jesum selbst begraben" (Make my heart pure, I want to bury Jesus within me), "Denn er soll nunmehr in mir, für und für, Seine süsse Ruhe haben" (For from now on he will have a sweet resting place in me forever). "Welt geh aus, lass Jesum ein" (Depart world, let Jesus in).

In the Christmas Oratorio, one meets not only different themes but also different biblical images and allusions, and, at least in places, I detect a more consciously emotive language to describe the believer's relation to Christ. In the very first cantata for Christmas Day (there are six cantatas in the Christmas Oratorio, the last for Epiphany), the narration of the birth of Christ in Judea leads to a recitative in which Christ is called "mein liebster

Bräutigam" (my beloved bridegroom). This is followed by an alto aria that sings of receiving the "fairest one, beloved one" (den Schönsten, den Liebsten) "mit zärtlichen Trieben" (with tender longing), and ends with the words "eile den Bräutigam sehnlichst zu lieben" (hurry that you may love the bridegroom passionately).

Later, in the fourth cantata for the day of the circumcision of Christ, there is a haunting soprano-bass duet that begins as a recitative and becomes an arioso. Here Bach heightens the emotion by giving the text to two voices, male and female, which seem to merge into one as they sing to each other: "Mein Jesus soll mir immerfort vor meinen Augen schweben" (My Jesus will always hover in front of my eyes), "mein Jesus heiszet meine Lust" (my Jesus means my delight [or desire]), and "Komm, ich will dich mit Lust umfassen" (Come, I will seize you with delight), "mein Herze soll dich nimmer lassen, ach, so nimm mich zu dir" (my heart will never leave you, O, take me to yourself). And in the duet that follows: "So will ich dich entzücket nenne, wenn Brust und Herz zu dir vor Liebe brennen" (I will speak your name with rapture, since my breast and my heart are burning with love for you).

This is not the kind of language that Bach's fellow Lutherans (or any Christians) are accustomed to hear from the pulpit, at least not today. Indeed, one would have to look long and hard to find such affective language used to speak of Christian devotion in recent Lutheran devotional literature, perhaps in anything that has been written by Lutherans in this country in the last hundred years, or even longer.

Johann Sebastian Bach was born in 1685 and died in 1750, which means that he was a contemporary of the two formative figures in the history of pietism, Philip Jakob Spener (1635-1705) and August Hermann Francke (1663-1727). Spener's *Pia Desideria* was published in 1675, ten years before Bach's birth, and was avidly read by laity (and one hopes by the clergy as well) in the decades that followed. Written in response to the decline in morals and devotion in the Lutheran churches of Germany, *Pia Desideria* was a tract on reform with an emphasis on Bible reading, personal devotion, works of charity, and renewed emphasis on preaching, among other things.

There is, however, another side to pietism that is sometimes forgotten. Pietism did not simply call for a renewal and deepening of personal piety; it consciously sought to revive aspects of medieval piety that had been lost in the years since the Reformation. One of the books that formed Spener's piety as a youth was Johann Arndt's *True Christianity*, a Lutheran devotional treatise written at the beginning of the seventeenth century that drew deeply on medieval spiritual writings. In the *Pia Desideria* Spener recommended that alongside of the Bible the devout Christian should read the writings of Johann Tauler, a medieval mystic, and the spiritual guide entitled *Theologia Germania* about which Luther had said: "No book except the Bible and St. Augustine has come to my attention from which I have learned more about God, Christ, man and all things." He also mentioned Thomas à Kempis's *Imitation of Christ*, an anonymous work that was appended to the works of Ephraem the Syrian and, of course, "our dear Arndt," as he calls the author of *True Christianity*.[1]

Johann Arndt was born in 1555. He first studied medicine, but after recovering from an illness he began the study of theology, first at Helmstaedt and later at Wittenberg. In 1584 he became a pastor in Badeborn, and later he moved to St. Nicholas Church in Quedlinburg. Like others in his day he was involved in the theological controversies spawned by the Reformation, but his true love was the life of prayer and devotion, what we today call spirituality. In 1597 he edited Luther's version of the *Theologia Germania* with a long introduction; and a few years later he reprinted it along with the *Imitatio Christi*. He also edited Johann Staupitz's *De amore dei* in a German version.

In the same year he published the first of his four books of *True Christianity*, a work that was to prove extraordinarily popular.[2] During his lifetime it was reprinted twenty times, translated into other languages, including English, and by the end of the eighteenth century it had gone through 125 reprintings. I was once told by Leigh Jordahl, a historian at Luther College, that along with the Bible and Luther's Small Catechism and a hymnal, immigrants were almost sure to have Arndt's *True Christianity* tucked away somewhere in a trunk or knapsack among the possessions they carried to this country.

At the very beginning of his work Arndt addresses the reader as follows: "[I wish to show] that we bear the name of Christ not only because we ought to believe in Christ, but also because we are to live in Christ and

---

1. See Philip Jacob Spener, *Pia Desideria*, trans. and ed. Theodore G. Tappert (Philadelphia, 1964), pp. 111-12.
2. For an English translation see *Johann Arndt: True Christianity*, trans. and with an introduction by Peter Erb (New York: Paulist Press, 1979).

he in us."[3] This language is, of course, unexceptional; it is found in the Gospel of John and in St. Paul, and in the works of Martin Luther. Yet his choice of words is not accidental. In the Christian life, he says, faith is not enough; Christ must live *in* us and we must live *in* him, that is, be joined to him in love. As one looks closely at Arndt's language, his use of the Gospel of John and of the First Epistle of John, for example 1 John 3:2, "we will be like [God]," as well as 2 Peter 1:4, "partakers of divine nature" (the classic text for the Greek doctrine of *theosis*), the bride and bridegroom imagery, his accent on growth in holiness, and the central place he gives to the love *for* God in the Christian life, it is apparent that the controlling idea behind *True Christianity* is union with Christ: "By . . . deep trust and heartfelt assent, [the believer] gives his heart completely and utterly to God, rests in God alone, gives himself over to God, clings to God alone, unites himself with God, is a participant of all that which is God and Christ, becomes one spirit with God."[4]

In Arndt, as in all spiritual writers, the movement of God toward human beings is complemented by a movement of the believer toward God, a raising up, an ascent, which is propelled by love and longing for God. Love is the basis for fellowship and union with God. "The end of all theology and Christianity is union with God . . . marriage with the heavenly bridegroom Jesus Christ."[5]

Johann Arndt was not alone in his conviction that in the wake of the Reformation key aspects of the spiritual tradition had been lost. Another spiritual writer was John Gerhard (1582-1637), the great Lutheran scholastic theologian, who was a friend and disciple of Arndt. Besides his massive dogmatic theology, the *Loci,* he also wrote a devotional work entitled *Meditationes Sacrae,* which was almost as popular as Arndt's book. There was also Philip Nicolai (1556-1608), a pastor in Unna/Westfalen and later in Hamburg, and the author of two of our most beloved hymns: "Wie schön leuchtet der Morgenstern" and "Wachet auf, ruft uns die Stimme." Valerius Herberger (1562-1627), a pastor in Poland, and the German pastor Stephan Praetorius (1536-1603) both wrote devotional works in the same spirit, often drawing on the same sources. For Praetorius, "holiness" and "sharing

---

3. Foreword to *True Christianity;* in Erb, ed., p. 21.
4. *True Christianity* 1.5; in Erb, ed., p. 45.
5. Preface to the *Theologia Deutsch;* cited in Erb's introduction to *True Christianity,* p. 9.

in the divine nature" were more congenial terms with which to speak about the Christian life than *simul iustus et peccator*. Christian growth required penultimate goals.

Bach's piety then, at least as reflected in a few arias from the Christmas Oratorio, cannot be simply attributed to the influence of pietism. He drew from much deeper sources, as did his contemporaries. The very title of Spener's book is noteworthy. He called it *Pia Desideria,* pious or godly desires or yearning. The Latin word *desiderium* is a venerable term in Christian tradition. It can, of course, be used in a pejorative sense to designate evil desires or concupiscence, for example, "control your body in holiness and honor, not with lustful passion [*non in passione desiderii]*" (1 Thess. 4:5), but more often it is used positively, as for example in this passage from Augustine's *Homilies on the First Epistle of John*. Augustine is commenting on 1 John 3:2: "Beloved, we are God's children now; what we will be has not yet been revealed. What we do know is this: when he is revealed, we will be like him, for we will see him as he is." Augustine asks: What shall we be, when we shall see God? In this life we cannot know what it will be like to see God; therefore

> because you cannot see at present, let your vocation be found in desire [*desiderium*]. The whole life of a good Christian is a holy desire [*sanctum desiderium;* one is tempted to think that Spener got the title of his book from this passage]. What you long for, as yet you do not see; but longing makes in you the room that shall be filled, when that which you are to see shall come. When you would fill a purse, knowing how large a present it is to hold, you stretch wide its cloth or leather; knowing how much you are to put in it, and seeing that the purse is small, you extend it to make more room. So by withholding the vision God extends the longing, through longing he makes the soul extend, by extending it he makes room in it.[6]

No doubt one reason Spener chose the title *Pia desideria* was that the work focused on the central place of the affections in the Christian life. This is a truth so self-evident that one wonders why it is so often forgotten. Recall the opening words of Jonathan Edwards's treatise *The Religious Affections:* "The holy Scriptures," he writes, "do everywhere place religion very

---

6. Augustine, *Tractatus on 1 John* 4.6.

much in the affections; such as fear, hope, love, hatred, desire, joy, sorrow, gratitude, compassion, and zeal."[7]

Already in the third century, Lactantius, an early Latin apologist sometimes called the Christian Cicero, had chided the Stoics for ignoring the role that mercy, pity, desire, and fear play in human action. Such things they call "diseases of the soul" *(morbos animi)*. The Stoics, he writes, take away from us all the "affections by the impulse of which the soul is moved."[8] In this passage, Lactantius is taking sides in a long-standing debate, signaled by his use of the Aristotelian term "move." Aristotle had argued that knowing what is right or wrong is not enough; there must be something that moves us to do the good and to avoid evil. All action, he wrote, can be reduced to "thought" and "desire," for without a conception of what is to be done we do not know what it is we are to do, but without desire, something that draws us to the object and keeps our sights firmly fixed on it, there is no possibility of movement. "The proximate reason for movement," writes Aristotle, "is desire."[9]

A similar argument can be found in Gregory of Nyssa. In his treatise *De Anima et Resurrectione,* Gregory asks: Why were the passions (e.g., desire and fear) given to human beings in the first place? If they only work evil (as many assume), how can it be said that human beings are created in the image of God? That is, if the passions are inherently evil, then God created human beings imperfect, which is impossible and contrary to the clear words of Scripture.

Desire, says Gregory, is a "yearning for that which is lacking and a longing for enjoyment."[10] It is a faculty that is clearly observable in animal behavior, in, for example, procreation, in caring for young, in procuring food. Just as an animal has an instinctive drive (he uses Aristotle's word *orexis*) to acquire what is necessary for life, so also human beings have certain drives or impulses, for example, desire and fear, that were given for a good purpose. Whether they are put to the good ends for which they were created depends, of course, on how they are directed. If they are directed to a good end they can be instruments of virtue, but if they are directed to an evil end they become instruments of vice.

---

7. Jonathan Edwards, *The Religious Affections* 1.4.
8. Lactantius, *Divine Institutes* 6.14-15.
9. Aristotle, *On Movement* 701a35.
10. *Patrologia Graeca* (hereafter *PG*) 46, 57a.

Gregory assumes, of course, that it is not enough to know the good or to believe in God; one must be capable of holding fast to the good, of grasping it firmly, of clinging to it, of making it one's own. There must be something that binds us to God, and that, in the language of the Scriptures, is love. Hence Gregory asks: "What can draw us to fasten ourselves firmly to heavenly things," that is, to the good? Without love there is no way we can be united to God.[11] We must learn, in a happy phrase, the "*habit* of loving the beautiful."[12]

Gregory seizes on the word *love,* and though he uses the Greek term *agape,* it is clear that he means *eros,* love as yearning and desire. Like other Christian thinkers, Gregory has some uneasiness about using the conventional terms for desire, because of their dark side in the Scriptures, as in the passage from 1 Thessalonians cited earlier. The one place where Aristotle's term *desire (orexis)* is used is in the passage in Romans 1 where Paul speaks about "degrading passions": "men giving up natural intercourse with women, . . . consumed with passion [*orexei*] for one another" (1:26). By using *agape* instead of *desire* or *passion,* Gregory made it possible for Christians to appropriate the acquisitive side of love while at the same time using the language of the Bible.

For some this may appear to be a bit of chicanery, a sleight of hand, but it should not be forgotten that terms for desire are used regularly in the Scriptures to speak about our relation to God. "Whom have I in heaven but you? There is nothing on earth that I *desire* besides you" (Ps. 73:25). "As a hart longs for flowing streams, so *longs* my soul for you, O God" (Ps. 42:1).[13] How this language should be interpreted was a matter of discussion already in antiquity. Pseudo-Dionysius had to defend his use of the term *eros.* "Do not think," he says, "that in giving status to the term 'yearning' [*eros*] I am running counter to Scripture." In what seems a deliberately playful passage, he explains how the language of love works in the Scriptures. For example, he asks what one is to make of this passage from Proverbs about Wisdom (which for Dionysius was Christ): "Desire [*erastheti*] her and she shall hold you; exalt her and she will extol you" (4:8). The careful reader of the Bible will discover, he

11. *PG* 56, 65a.

12. *PG* 46, 93c.

13. Bernard: "Virtue is that by which one seeks eagerly for the Creator and when one finds him, holds to him with all one's might." *On Loving God* 2.2; in *Bernard of Clairvaux: Selected Works,* ed. and trans. G. R. Evans (New York, 1987), p. 176.

continues, that in places the Scriptures use the term *agape* when they mean desire or erotic love, implying that this is the case in other passages. His example comes from the Septuagint version of 2 Samuel 1, David's lament over Jonathan, at the end of which, speaking of the love between them, he cries out: "Your love for me was greater than love for women." Here where one would expect to find the term *eros* the Scriptures use *agapesis*. From this Dionysius concludes: "To those listening properly to the divine things the term 'love' is used by the sacred writers in divine revelation with the exact same meaning as the term 'eros.'"[14]

By giving *eros*, and hence the affections, a place in Christian discourse, Christian thinkers were able to emphasize that fellowship with God was the goal of Christian life. As Dionysius says in this passage, love signifies a "capacity to bring about unity, an alliance." The eastern Christian notion of *theosis* (divinization) really means participation through love in the divine life, as can be seen in a writer such as Maximus the Confessor.

Like Augustine and Gregory, Maximus knew the destructive power of the passions, and he recognized that they could simply be dismissed as evil impulses. At the very beginning of his work *Quaestiones ad Thalassium*, brief essays on the interpretation of difficult biblical texts, he asks: Are the passions evil in themselves, or do they become evil by use? By passions he means desire and fear, pleasure and pain. His answer is that the passions are evil only if they are put to the service of evil ends; what is more, they can — indeed, must — have a positive role in the life of faith. "The passions can become good when a devout person turns away from earthly things and gives himself wholly to heavenly things." Hence, desire, or love, can bring about a "yearning for divine things," and pleasure can mean "the quiet enjoyment the mind finds in contemplating divine things."[15] For Maximus the spiritual life has to do with constancy, with learning over a long period of time to focus one's thoughts, to discipline one's body, to channel one's affections so that they remain fixed on God. Anyone who prays seriously, and not just in times of distress or need, knows that the largest obstacle to prayer is distracting thoughts, the inability of the human mind to be quiet and to give itself to God.

14. *The Divine Names* 4.11-12, in *Pseudo-Dionysius: The Complete Works*, trans. Colm Luibheid (New York, 1987), pp. 80-81.

15. Maximus, *Quaestiones ad Thalassium* 1, ed. Carl Laga and Carlos Steel, in *Corpus Christianorum*, Series Graeca 7 (1980), pp. 47-49.

Maximus sums up early Christian thinking on the affections and anticipates the rich and redolent language of later spiritual writers — and, one might add, of Bach. Knowledge of God "without passion" does not move the mind, because such knowledge is simply the "mere thought of a thing." Knowledge must be accompanied by "the blessed passion of holy love, which binds the mind to spiritual realities and persuades it to prefer the immaterial to the material and the intelligible and divine to sensible things." Although it is possible to detect the influence of classical thought, particularly Aristotle, on Christian thinking about the passions, after reading Maximus one comes away with the sense that something radically new has been unleashed there. The old vessels have difficulty containing the new wine. In places his language is rapturous. He says things such as this: "For the mind of one who is continuallly in the presence of God even his concupiscence abounds beyond measure into a divine desire." All human beings are *moved* by a passionate desire to know God and to hold on to God. "Let our reason therefore be *moved* to seek God, and let the power of desire bring us to long for him."[16]

Of course, with Maximus I have moved far beyond Bach and Lutheran pietism. But my purpose is not to trace influences. What Bach knew, however, whether through experience, study of the Bible, or reading John Arndt, was what many other Christians knew, that love for God was as necessary as God's love for us. There can, of course, only be love for God where one has first been loved by God; but being loved is not enough. Gregory of Nyssa spoke of the love for God as a "reciprocating love," a love that invites love in the one who is loved. It is only as we love that we are able to give ourselves. Love lifts us out of ourselves, turns our minds and hearts to the one who loves us, and prevents faith from becoming self-centered and self-authenticating. Love seeks to possess, to embrace, to delight in the beloved. In Augustine's words taken from Psalm 73, "for me to cleave to God is good" *(mihi adhaerere Deo bonum est)*.[17]

Within early Lutheran history, as I have already observed, the other major figure besides Arndt who saw the place of love for God in Christian

16. *Centuries on Charity* 2.48, 66-67, trans. G. Berthold, in *Maximus the Confessor: Selected Writings* (New York, 1985), pp. 53, 70-71; *Commentary on the Lord's Prayer,* in the same volume, p. 113.

17. See, for example, *De Trinitate* 6.5.7; *On the Spirit and the Letter* 22.37; and *City of God* 10.3.

life was Johann Gerhard. Gerhard, it should be noted, was a serious student of the church fathers and the medievals. His *loci* are filled with patristic citations, and he wrote the first patrology, that is, a book providing an account of the life, writings, and thought of the *doctores ecclesiae* from the beginning until the Middle Ages. To this day the term *patrology* is still used for such a work.

The ninth meditation in his *Sacrae meditationes* is entitled *"De amando solo Deo,"* and its theme is "by love the believer cleaves to God." Reading through this brief meditation one can detect the influence of St. Augustine, St. Gregory, and St. Bernard, and other formative thinkers in the church's history. In the first sentence he says that our telos as human beings is to "love that chief good . . . without whom there is no other good," for no creature can satisfy our "desire." He dwells first on God's love for us, the sending of Christ as redeemer, using the terms *dilectio* and *diligo*, then abruptly he switches to *amo* and begins speaking of our love for God. His point is that God's love for us would come to naught if it did not engender our love for God in return. "Without the love for God you can never come to the saving knowledge of God." For to know God is to partake of God, to be transformed by God, to be united with God. "Love is the chief thing that unites us to God [*summum vinculum*], because the one who loves and that which is loved become one." Love for God is the "chariot of Elijah which ascends to heaven," the "seal" by which God seals believers. "For faith itself, the sole cause of our justification, is not genuine, unless it shows itself in love [for God]. There is not true faith unless there is firm trust; and there is no trust without the love of God."[18]

Expanding on this theme, Gerhard cites two biblical texts, Ephesians 3:17, "God dwells in our hearts by faith," and Romans 5:5, "God's love has been poured into our hearts through the Holy Spirit that has been given to us." The citation of Romans 5 in this context is striking, for Gerhard is drawing on a tradition of interpretation that goes back to St. Augustine. The conventional reading of Romans 5 is that the phrase "love of God" refers to God's love for us. Yet Augustine took the passage to refer to our love for God (the Greek could be read either way), and he did so consistently. In his view the text is speaking about the gift of the Holy Spirit, and love is the premier gift of the Spirit. Hence when St. Paul says that love

18. John Gerhard, *Sacrae Meditationes,* Meditatio 9 (London, 1672), pp. 30-35.

89

has been "poured into our hearts," Augustine understands this to be a gift that we possess, not the basis for the gift.

Without this gift our hearts are cold and lifeless, unable to delight in God and love our neighbor. When we receive this bounty in our hearts we "are fired to cleave to [the] creator." For Augustine, as well as for Gerhard and Arndt, Paul's words in Romans were to be understood in tandem with another passage, 1 John 4:13: "By this we know that we abide in him and he in us, because he has given us of his Spirit." From here Augustine is led to explore the indwelling of the Holy Trinity within us, which is a central theme in John Arndt's *True Christianity*, particularly in book five. Our love for God is God's gift to us that is poured into our hearts by the Holy Spirit.

But that is a topic for another essay. It is time now to draw some conclusions. I did not hear the name Johann Arndt until I had left seminary, and John Gerhard I knew only as a dogmatic theologian. Several years after graduation I discovered Arndt, and I remember on a visit with my former homiletics professor, Richard Caemmerer, I asked him what he thought of Arndt. He simply blurted out: "Oh, he was a pietist!" That, apparently, was enough to dismiss him from serious consideration. Well, whatever this remark suggests about Caemmerer's attitude to pietism, it is somewhat anachronistic to call someone who was born in 1555 (Spener, the founder of the pietist movement, was born in 1635) a pietist. Something else, as we have seen, was at work in his life and thought, as it was in the devotional works of Gerhard. Yet Caemmerer's instinct may have been sound in yoking these early Lutheran devotional writers with the later pietists.

Whatever one wishes to call these strands of Lutheran spirituality, there can be no question that their piety grew out of a genuinely biblical and hence authentically Catholic impulse. In giving priority to the love for God in the Christian life, they set forth a vision of the Christian life, as did St. Paul and St. John, in which the Christ for us was perfected by the Christ in us, and not least, they inspired the faithful to pursue a life of holiness as does the Bible. Every section of the New Testament — St. Paul, the Johannine literature, the Synoptic Gospels (Sermon on the Mount), Hebrews, and 1 Peter — gives a central place to the pursuit of holiness. Consider 2 Corinthians 7:1: "Since we have these promises [I will live in them and move among them and I will be their God], let us cleanse ourselves from every defilement of body and spirit, and make holiness perfect in fear of God." Or 1 Peter 1:15-16: "Be holy yourself in all your conduct; for it is written, 'You shall be holy, for I am holy.' " Parenthetically, one might add

that the theology underlying these early Lutheran spiritual writings provided a firm biblical basis for the doing of good works.

The spiritual world they presented to Lutheran readers was not the
product of deformed late medieval piety (if there ever was such a thing);
it was the fruit of centuries of Christian thought and experience based on
the Scriptures and informed by the central articles of faith — namely, the
two natures of Christ and the doctrine of the Holy Trinity — and by the
sacraments. Indeed, one might press the point to argue that it was *because*
they drew on the spiritual traditions of the medieval world, which were, of
course, nurtured by the spiritual writers of the early church, that these early
pietists were so biblical.

Nevertheless, no matter how pure its sources, laudable its aims, inspired its proponents, Lutheran pietism has not lived on, and where it has
endured it has been transformed into something else, forgetful of its roots.
It is tempting to use pietism as a metaphor for the Lutheran tradition as a
whole. Just as the writings of Spener and Francke were not enough to sustain
a genuine piety, so the writings of Luther and the Augsburg Confession are
not enough to transmit the Catholic faith confessed in the Creeds. Spener
cannot take the place of Arndt, just as Arndt cannot take the place of St.
Bernard and Bernard cannot take the place of Maximus or Augustine; so
Luther cannot take the place of St. Thomas, just as Thomas cannot take
the place of Gregory the Great, or Athanasius, or Irenaeus. Without the
support of the whole, the parts cannot stand.

The Lutheran reformation, though conservative, doctrinal, churchly,
and sacramental, was nevertheless partial and one-sided. What it saw it
grasped with freshness and power; but its brilliant vision could also be
blinding. For in the very act of repossessing it began a process of dispos-
sessing. Tragically, the Reformation sundered the church's memory and cut
off the Reformation traditions from much that was precious in the church's
faith and life. Without the nourishment of Catholic piety, Lutheran pietism,
whether in the version of Arndt or of Spener, was doomed to extinction.
Lutheranism is not the whole and was never intended to be the whole, and
the Reformation heritage cannot survive if it ignores the Catholic tradition.

The early Lutheran spiritual writers, John Arndt and John Gerhard,
remind us that the first commandment is: "You shall love the Lord your
God with all your heart and with all your soul and with all your might."
From this they draw the obvious conclusion: loving God is the beginning
and the end of the Christian life, and Christian life is about the ordering

91

of one's loves. "Where your treasure is, there will your heart be also." Christian faith is as much a matter of what one loves as it is of what one believes or what one does. For the gift that God desires is the gift of ourselves, and there is no giving of the self that is not a giving of the heart. St. Augustine wrote: "We offer to him, on the altar of the heart, the sacrifice of humility and praise, and the flame on the altar is the burning fire of love. To see him as he can be seen and to cleave to him, we purify ourselves from every stain of sin and evil desire and we consecrate ourselves in his name. For he himself is the source of our bliss, he himself is the goal of all our striving. . . . For we direct our course towards him with love so that in reaching him we may find our rest, and attain our happiness because we have achieved our fulfillment in him."[19]

19. Augustine, *City of God* 10.3.

The Church Is
a Communion of Churches

Günther Gassmann

Introduction

OUR TITLE states a thesis and a task or goal: "The church is a communion of churches." It is a *thesis* in that it proposes a fundamental ecclesiological perspective: The church universal, or the church of Jesus Christ, *is* a communion of local churches (local could be in the sense of a congregation or diocese or even national church, which in itself could be understood as a communion of local churches). The church universal is not made up of or composed by the addition of local churches. Rather, it exists, is present, in these local churches and finds its universal, catholic manifestation in the *koinonia* of these churches. "The church *is* a communion of churches."

The theme also expresses a task and goal. It is the goal of all our ecumenical endeavors that the unity of the church should find its visible manifestation in the form of a communion of churches. Sometimes we call this a "full communion" of churches, which presupposes and is expressed in agreement in faith, mutual recognition, reconciliation, sharing of ordained ministries and sacraments, forms of common deliberations and decision making, and common witness and service in the world. It is a full communion of churches belonging to different confessional traditions, and it can also be envisioned as a communion of Christian world communions.

This goal is not just before us. The churches in the last few decades have taken significant steps on the way toward this goal. Forms of a real, though still imperfect, communion already exist between the churches —

as Pope John Paul II and others have stated repeatedly. This reality of communion, based on radical changes in twentieth-century church history, is simply ignored by those interpreters of present ecumenism who stare in a simplistic way at ecumenical progress, noticing only the big jumps forward and accordingly speaking of stagnation or standstill when they don't see such rapid progress. Of course, we would like to see more ecumenical commitment and activity as a regular element in the life of the churches. But the ecumenical movement is indeed moving, often in the quiet development of changed attitudes and relationships on local levels, and also quite frequently in new and significant initiatives like the ones to be considered and voted on by the Evangelical Lutheran Church in America in 1997, or like the recently published encyclical letter of John Paul II, *Ut Unum Sint.* In all these ecumenical efforts the task remains, and the goal gives direction to the task: to move toward the unity of the church in the form of a communion of churches.

A central term in this title, thesis, and task is "communion" *(koinonia).* Why has the term "communion" become so prominent in recent ecclesiological and ecumenical discussion? Wherein lies the theological and ecclesiological potential of this concept?

The Emergence and Significance of the Concept of Communion *(Koinonia)*

The concept of communion as an interpretation of the nature, mission, and unity of the church is, of course, not a new one. It has been used in different ways throughout church history. But one thing seems clear: the last decades have seen increased reference to this concept and more frequent integration of this concept into ecclesiological and ecumenical texts. This has happened especially in Roman Catholic, Orthodox, and in part also Anglican thinking.

The Second Vatican Council played an important role in the shift from the remnants of an earlier predominantly juridical, institutional ecclesiology to an ecclesiology of the people of God in salvation and secular history, that is, to an ecclesiology of communion (*post festum* perhaps overemphasized in the report of the Extraordinary Bishops' Synod in 1985 as *the* guiding perspective of the Council). Already in 1962 Father Jérome Hamér published a book with a title nearly identical with the title of this chapter: *The Church Is a Communion (L'Église est une communion)*. In 1979 our Episcopal friends published a report of an ecumenical study with a similarly programmatic title: "A Communion of Communions." Bilateral dialogues on the international level received the communion concept into their deliberations and made it a leading perspective — for example, in the Final Report of the Anglican–Roman Catholic International Commission (ARCIC; 1981); in the following reports of ARCIC like "Salvation and the Church" (1987) and "The Church as Communion" (1991); in the Reformed–Roman Catholic dialogue report: "Towards a Common Understanding of the Church" (1990); in the Munich Statement of the Orthodox–Roman Catholic dialogue on "The Mystery of the Church and the Eucharist in the Light of the Mystery of the Holy Trinity" (1982); and now also in the Lutheran–Roman Catholic report on "Church and Justification" (1993).

Also in the World Council of Churches, and especially in the work of the Faith and Order Commission, the concept of communion/*koinonia* has become a major perspective in recent years. We find first traces of the concept in the *Baptism, Eucharist and Ministry* document (e.g., p. 19). It was highlighted in the title (and content) of the statement of the 1991 Canberra Assembly of the WCC on "The Unity of the Church as Koinonia: Gift and Calling." Here, communion/*koinonia* was introduced as an interpretation and clarification of the term "unity." The term "unity," though in a way indispensable, has lost much of its importance in ecumenical circles because of its political misuse (in Eastern Europe and some Third World countries) and its possible misinterpretation in terms of uniformity, or centralized or undifferentiated and colorless unity. Such diffuse unity is experienced sometimes in united churches that lack a clear theological, confessional, and ecclesiological profile. However, this is a danger not only for united churches of formerly different denominations but also for united churches formed by churches of the same confession.

Two years after the Canberra statement on unity as *koinonia*, the Fifth World Conference on Faith and Order (1993) at Santiago de Compostela in Spain made communion/*koinonia* part of the title and the focus of much of the deliberations of the World Conference: "Towards Koinonia in Faith, Life and Witness." The Conference represents without doubt the most intensive and comprehensive explication and application of the concept of communion in relation to the understanding of the church and its unity. This explication is developed in terms of the foundation of unity as communion in the one apostolic *faith*, in terms of the sacramental, spiritual, and ministerial *life* of communion, and in terms of the mission of the communion as sign and instrument of God's purpose for humanity and creation *(witness)*.

In these bilateral and multilateral dialogue reports and other texts, a wealth of reflection on communion/*koinonia* is now available to us. We have become aware of the danger of using the term "communion" too widely and generally, the danger of its becoming a slogan. At the same time we recognize the obvious usefulness of "communion" for describing what we mean by "church" and what we mean by "church unity."

Why has communion become such a central concept in present ecclesiological and ecumenical thinking? A few indications must suffice.

(1) The concept of communion is best suited to *comprehend and integrate* in a consistent manner the many and various elements of ecclesiology: the divine and human, the vertical and horizontal, the Old and New Testament witness, the local and universal, oneness and diversity, the nature and mission of the Church. These and other elements and perspectives can be held together and related to each other by the concept of communion in a way that no other concept is able to do.

(2) Accordingly, the concept of communion indicates a *deeper theological and spiritual meaning* of our vision of the church than terms such as "community" or "fellowship" or even "church" itself can convey.

(3) By interrelating in an integral way the *divine and human nature* of the church, the concept of communion helps to overcome the Protestant tendency to regard the church primarily in historical, sociological, and organizational (or even managerial) terms. Communion may also overcome the contrasting Eastern Orthodox tendency to see the church so exclusively as a divine reality that an awareness is lacking of the failures, disobedience, and need for renewal of the church in its historical forms of existence.

(4) The term "communion" helps to reinterpret the goal of the *visible unity* of the church in a way that avoids the negative connotations of the term "unity" that were mentioned above. At the same time the historical character of the unity we seek — its dynamic nature, its inclusion of diversity, and the possibility to consider unity as a coming together of worldwide Christian communions — can be much more adequately expressed by "communion" than by "unity."

(5) The concept of communion responds to the widespread *contemporary yearning for community* in church and society. We live in a time of

increasing individualism, loneliness, and imposed egotism because of the mechanisms of societies geared toward success, achievement, competition, and status. The concept of communion, when offered in appropriate realizations (and not simply as a concept), may assist in renewing forms of church life so that these not only provide a "home" for believers but also radiate a sense and experience of community that will be attractive and inviting to people outside the churches.

The Biblical Sources and Implications of Communion/*Koinonia*

Whatever reasons we may find for the new prominence of the concept of communion/*koinonia,* a sufficient biblical basis and usage of this concept will be essential. This does not mean that we should simply look for every occurrence of the word *koinonia* and its related forms in the Bible. Rather, we may draw out contours of a *koinonia* dimension in the framework of which other terms can be interpreted.

As with other issues, we do not find in the New Testament texts a developed, systematic concept of *koinonia*/communion. The term *koinonia* was taken over from a Greek and Roman cultural and socioreligious context and was filled and reappropriated with the new content of the Christian faith. The different usages of *koinonia* in the New Testament, when connected with each other in their complementary meanings, provide for us an orientation for our understanding of *koinonia*/communion.

In Paul *koinonia* is closely related to the three persons of the Trinity: it has its foundation in God's call of the faithful into the *koinonia* of (or with) his Son, Jesus Christ (1 Cor. 1:9), and this *koinonia* is blessed by the communion of and in the Holy Spirit (2 Cor. 13:14). Those who are in communion with Christ receive on Christ's account righteousness from God through faith and participate in the *koinonia* of Christ's suffering and death in order to receive the promise of the resurrection from the dead (Phil. 3:8-11). In the Lord's Supper the partakers have *koinonia* with the blood of Christ and in the body of Christ (1 Cor. 10:16). This communion makes the many who participate in it *one* body (1 Cor. 10:17). The communion thus established can also be described as *koinonia* in the gospel (Phil. 1:5) and *koinonia* in faith (Philem. 6). One expression of this *koinonia* is the sharing of spiritual goods in mission

97

and teaching (Gal. 6:6) and the sharing of material goods in the local church and among local churches (Rom. 15:26-27, collection for Jerusalem). In this context *koinonia* forms the basis of the relationship between Gentile and Jewish Christian churches (Gal. 2:9-10).

Other New Testament writings describe *koinonia* in similar ways in various contexts as an expression of the essential interrelation between God's communion with believers and the believers' communion with one another (e.g., 1 John 1; Heb. 2:14; 2 Pet. 1:4). Acts 2:42 describes *koinonia* in the comprehensive framework of the apostles' teaching, sacramental fellowship, and shared prayer, leading then also to the sharing of possessions and goods across social boundaries.

According to the New Testament witness, *koinonia*/communion is not the creation of Christians. It is a gift of the triune God that enables participation and sharing in the divine life, divine gifts, and divine active presence for the forgiveness of sins and faith. This *koinonia* with God is lived out in the *koinonia* among those who believe. Both dimensions are inextricably linked. The communion among believers is centered in worship and especially the eucharist. *Koinonia* shapes all aspects of the life of the community, from the sharing of faith and confession and spiritual gifts to the sharing of material goods. *Koinonia* thus interconnects the divine foundation of the church with the quality of its life and mission in history.

Major Aspects of Communion for Ecclesiology

How can the New Testament understanding of *koinonia* as communion, community, participation, partaking, and having in common shed a new light on basic elements of our understanding of the Christian faith and especially the church? And how can these different elements be interrelated and integrated with one another in order to avoid one-sided perspectives of ecclesiology? Let us look at a number of such elements from the perspective of a Lutheran and ecumenical ecclesiology.

Communion as Fundamental for the God-Human Relationship

The fundamental dimension of the Christian faith is the relationship between God and human beings, between God and humanity. This relationship can be expressed in terms of communion. It is, as always, a communion freely established and given by God. It has its basis in God's creation and in the dignity given to human persons as created in the image of God, co-creators with God, responding in faith to God, responsible to God for their life and actions. This communion has been broken on the human side; human sin consists basically and precisely in the refusal to accept communion with God and to remain faithful to that communion.

God has given this communion a corporate form in the covenants of the Old Testament. These covenants are based on mutual faithfulness between God and his people, but also on a just communion among the people in obedience to the divine will (law). We see here a kind of anticipation or foreshadowing of the concept of *koinonia*/communion with its interlocking divine-human (vertical) and intrahuman (horizontal) dimensions. Human disobedience and sin have broken the intrahuman communion by injustice, oppression, and exploitation, just as they have betrayed the covenant communion with God by turning to other gods and idols. But God has remained faithful and has reestablished communion again and again.

This continuity of God's faithfulness links the communion of the Old Covenant with the communion of the New Testament. This new communion is reestablished through Christ's obedient and costly love to the Father, representing all sinful human beings on the cross and taking them through the resurrection to new life. Through Christ's act of reconciliation, communion with God is renewed in the power of the Holy Spirit. It is now offered to all peoples through the gospel in word and sacrament, and it is embraced by those who believe in Christ. Communion remains the fundamental individual and corporate expression of the relationship between God and believers.

Communion as the Ecclesial Dimension of Justification by Faith

That communion is the fundamental expression of the God-human relationship is further underlined by the doctrine and reality of justification by grace and by faith alone. Communion can be interpreted as the corporate or ecclesial expression and scope of justification — a perspective not too common for Lutherans.

Of course, justification refers first of all to the act of accounting and making righteous before God of individual persons. Individual sinful, ego-centered persons are liberated by Christ from their bondage to themselves. They are reconciled to God by the blood of Christ, by their mysteriously intimate relationship with Christ in the "happy exchange" of their sins with his grace and blamelessness (Luther). Thus communion between God and human persons is reestablished by sheer grace, gratuitously, and received by faith.

And there we have left it very often. But the connection between communion and justification in the context of the fundamental God-human relationship defines the reestablished communion of the justified with God as an ecclesial, corporate consequence of justification. All those thus made righteous (i.e., not primarily morally better, but set into a right relationship with God, which has moral consequences), and having received grace and forgiveness through word and sacrament, are linked together in a communion not of their own choice and making. They are bonded together by the triune God in a congregation or communion of saints, of justified sinners. God's communion with us is reestablished by the reconciling act of justification, which at the same time establishes the communion of the justified ones. In this sense communion expresses the corporate, ecclesial dimension of justification. What we have described is nothing else than an explication of Articles IV and VII of the Augsburg Confession in the perspective of communion and justification.

Communion as Grounded in the Trinity

We have, in fact, pointed out that the church is grounded in the action of the triune God in justification transmitted to faith by word and sacrament. The church comes about wherever communion with God the Father is reestablished through the saving work of Christ and is made an experienced reality in faithful living by the Holy Spirit. Communion in and with God, communion in and with Christ, and communion in the Holy Spirit are thus intimately interrelated; they are one single reality. As a consequence, the concept of communion helps us to understand the close connections within trinitarian images of the church, such as people of God, body of Christ, and temple of the Holy Spirit. These connections are so close that one could say that these images are explications of the concept of communion and that the concept of communion is an explication of these images. In its double orientation of communion with God and, based on that, communion among the faithful, the concept of communion helps us better understand the analogous double orientation of these images: communion *with* God and *among* God's people; communion *with* Christ and *among* the members of his body; communion *in* the Holy Spirit and *among* those gifted by the Spirit.

An additional dimension of the relationship between church and Trinity could be indicated. It refers to the inner-trinitarian, immanent communion of love, equality, and diversity among the three persons of the Godhead. Should not this *koinonia* of oneness in diversity be seen as an *Urbild,* a formative image for the nature of the communion of the church?

The Communion Structure of the Life of the Church

The communion structure of the life of the church is based on and sustained by the divine institutions of the Word of God, the sacraments, and the ordained ministry, which serves word and sacrament. The proclamation of the Word, of the gospel, builds up the communion of those who come to faith by accepting God's word of forgiveness and promise. The trinitarian act of baptism incorporates the baptized into the communion of the church. In the eucharist, in holy communion, the partakers share in the communion of Christ's body and blood and are thereby made into a communion of love and sharing with each other. The ordained ministry, set into the context of the communion of the many gifts and ministries of the people of God, serves the upbuilding of communion through word and sacrament and pastoral care. The episcopal ministry of pastoral oversight and leadership is not just a practical arrangement for good order, coordination, and administrative leadership. Such an episcopal ministry is an ecclesiological necessity if we want to move beyond congregationalism set within larger administrative units called synods or national churches. An episcopal ministry is an ecclesiological necessity because the church, understood also as a communion of congregations within a synod, diocese, or national church, needs the service and leadership of a special ministry set apart for this task. A ministry with such a scope would not only serve the faith, coherence, and unity of such wider geographical forms of ecclesial communion; it would also serve, together with synodical or conciliar instruments of deliberation and decision making, the unity between the different synods or dioceses of a national church and represent this church to other churches.

101

Thus an episcopal ministry should be conceived and structured from this ecclesiological perspective in the horizon of communion and not simply as a practical device for leadership or for halfhearted ecumenical accommodation.

Served, sustained, and shaped by these instituted and therefore institutional means, the inner life of the communion is marked by

- the mutual love, forgiveness, consolation, and support of the members of the communion as part of their general priesthood;
- the sharing of spiritual and material gifts not only within each community but also between communions in the framework of their worldwide communion;
- the interplay and complementarity of the gifts of the Holy Spirit that each member has received and that contribute to the life of the community;
- the inclusiveness and diversity of its membership, freely accepted and affirmed as God's rich created gifts, but transformed into a communion of oneness in diversity.

Since we use communion as an interpretation of what we mean by church, communion is also qualified by oneness, holiness, catholicity, and apostolicity. The church as communion on its different levels of expression is *one* by being grounded in the one God in trinitarian communion. This oneness in diversity is held together and is expressed in the common confession of the apostolic faith as witnessed to in Holy Scripture and as normatively confessed in the creeds of the early church and the confessions of the Reformation. This oneness is also manifested in the mutual recognition and sharing of the sacraments and the ordained ministry, in structures of common deliberation and decision making, and in joint witness and service to all people.

The church as communion is *holy* because it is allowed to have a share in God's unattainable holiness through which in the power of the Holy Spirit the members of the communion are sanctified. They are united in receiving holy gifts for their spiritual fellowship; they are bonded together in prayer, worship, and praise of the One who is the source and goal of their being-in-communion.

The church as communion is *catholic* because it is a universal communion of communions that lives in a diversity of social, cultural, and political contexts and with a diversity of spiritual, conceptual, and theological expressions. This catholic communion is held together by the commitment to and confession of the one apostolic faith and other instruments of unity.

The church as communion in this relationship of universality and particularity is, finally and decisively, an *apostolic* communion. It is not only a catholic, universal communion in space, but also a communion in time, a communion that has been and will remain until the eschatological judgment on its faithfulness and the fulfillment of its calling. The church as communion is apostolic because it has its foundation in the faith and mission of the apostolic community and is called to live in continuity with and faithfulness to the apostolic faith, mission, worship, ministry, and service.

The concept of communion helps us to hold together and interrelate the institutional and internal, personal characteristics of communion that have often been set in opposition to each other, and it helps us to understand the marks of the church both as marks of each individual communion (local church) and as marks and criteria of the communion of the local communions with one another, as a "communion of churches."

Communion as Mission

The concept of communion is integrative and comprehensive also in the respect that it enables us to hold together an instrumental and noninstrumental understanding of the church and to avoid the frequent one-sided emphasis on an instrumental view. Much of what has been said about the inner life and the marks of communion is oriented toward the (noninstrumental) quality of spiritual, faithful, committed life of the members of a communion and of the relationship between communions in mutual love and support and for the praise and the glory of God. This orientation also includes, however, the painful awareness that our realizations of communion during the church's pilgrimage in history are always marked by imperfection, shortcomings, and failures, all crying out for corporate repentance and renewal. But wherever signs of an inner quality of life in community are present, a life that has its center in the worship and praise of the triune God, there a sure foundation is provided also for the mission of the communion, its God-willed instrumental character.

Being grounded in and nurtured by the communion with the triune God, the church is intrinsically bound up in communion with God's saving and transforming history from creation to fulfillment. In other words, the church is called to be a sign and instrument of God's purpose for all of humanity and creation. Communion thus transcends its boundaries, stretching out to all people in loving service and solidarity. And beyond this, communion has an eschatological dimension, anticipating and fore-shadowing by the quality of its life the communion God wills for all people. This eschatological, open character of communion should, however, be lived out in ways that do not obscure the contours of its identity as a communion assembled around God's word and sacrament.

Our understanding of communion as mission is thus based on the notion that the church as a communion of communions is sent into the world as a sign and instrument of God's saving and transforming purpose in Christ. This mission includes, among other things,

- inviting people into the Christian communion by proclaiming the gospel of God's saving action in Jesus Christ;
- the public and common confession of the apostolic faith in confronting all powers and ideologies that claim to order and direct all aspects of human life;
- the exposure and critique of inhuman, unjust, oppressive, and totalitarian situations;
- service and assistance to all people in need.

This wide, open horizon of communion should protect every communion of Christians from becoming provincial and inward-looking and thus failing to respond to God's call to mission.

In so far as the Church lives an authentic koinonia, faithful to doctrine, it is a "prophetic sign" pointing beyond itself to the fullness of the Kingdom of God.[1]

Until this kingdom is realized in its fullness through the coming again of the Son of God, all realizations of Christian communion will be provisional and imperfect, stained by human sin and disobedience. Yet because

1. Discussion paper for Santiago de Compostela, Official Report of the Fifth World Conference on Faith and Order, p. 276.

of God's continuing faithfulness and active presence in Christ through the Holy Spirit, this communion is blessed by being a communion of grace and hope, a sign and anticipation of the communion that God wills for all people.

Contributors

CARL E. BRAATEN. Director, Center for Catholic and Evangelical Theology; Co-editor, *Pro Ecclesia*.

JAMES R. CRUMLEY. Bishop Emeritus, Lutheran Church in America.

GÜNTHER GASSMANN. Former Director of the Commission on Faith and Order, World Council of Churches, Geneva.

ROBERT W. JENSON. St. Olaf College; Associate Director, Center for Catholic and Evangelical Theology; Co-editor, *Pro Ecclesia*.

FRANK C. SENN. Pastor, Immanuel Lutheran Church, Evanston, Illinois.

ROBERT L. WILKEN. University of Virginia; Past President, American Academy of Religion.

DAVID S. YEAGO. Lutheran Theological Southern Seminary, Columbia, South Carolina.